Greetings from Daytona Beach

A Mornings Catch at Seabreeze, Fla.

Snack Bar At The Patio

MENU

EL CORTEZ-MANOR • Seabreeze and Ocean Boulevards • DAYTONA BEACH, FLORIDA
Now SEABREEZE MANOR

Schiffer Publishing Ltd®

4880 Lower Valley Road, Atglen, Pennsylvania 19310

Donald D. Spencer

Other Schiffer Books by Donald D. Spencer
Greetings from Ormond Beach
Greetings from St. Augustine

Other Schiffer Books on Related Subjects
Schiffer Publishing, Ltd. has several postcard books of different cities. Please check our website for more information on them.

Designed by Mark David Bowyer
Type set in ZapfEllipt BT / Souvenir Lt BT

ISBN: 978-0-7643-2806-0
Printed in China

Published by Schiffer Publishing Ltd.
4880 Lower Valley Road
Atglen, PA 19310
Phone: (610) 593-1777; Fax: (610) 593-2002
E-mail: Info@schifferbooks.com

For the largest selection of fine reference books on this and related subjects, please visit our web site at **www.schifferbooks.com**
We are always looking for people to write books on new and related subjects. If you have an idea for a book please contact us at the above address.

This book may be purchased from the publisher.
Include $3.95 for shipping.
Please try your bookstore first.
You may write for a free catalog.

In Europe, Schiffer books are distributed by
Bushwood Books
6 Marksbury Ave.
Kew Gardens
Surrey TW9 4JF England
Phone: 44 (0) 20 8392-8585; Fax: 44 (0) 20 8392-9876
E-mail: info@bushwoodbooks.co.uk
Website: www.bushwoodbooks.co.uk
Free postage in the U.K., Europe; air mail at cost.

Contents

Introduction

This book is a factorial representation of the Daytona Beach area's history through the use of views and images from postcards of yesteryear. But you don't have to be a postcard buff to enjoy the scenes of a fine city like Daytona Beach, with so many of its citizens and residents appreciative of its history and the many wonderful buildings that have been here—and the surprising number that remain.

Old-timers often reminisce about the "good old days", and what better way to visit them but through postcards published by the millions and sent between family and friends at the turn of the Twentieth Century.

But, times change and, in people's blind rush toward the future, a sense of direction can be lost. Many cities have lost their architectural heritage through "urban renewal." Old buildings come down with little thought for the past. Except for parts of buildings reused in new structures on their sites, the bulldozer of today's technology completely removes any trace of past structures, and a record of our past is irretrievably destroyed.

For over 200 years, Daytona Beach has been, and continues to be, a unique combination of history, charm, and remarkable consistency. Consequently, this beautiful city presents pictorial connections with the past through a collection of original buildings, grounds and streets, which are easily accessible and frequently well preserved.

Does history live only in old dusty books sitting on out-of-the-way shelves? What if we could go back in time? What were things really like? With an illustrated book like this one, it is possible in one's mind to go back in time and walk the same streets. It is particularly pleasant to make the comparisons between what is here today and what existed in the same locations decades ago.

This book can be used as an addition to Daytona Beach's history or as a nostalgic tour through the city's past. It is a delightful stroll down memory lane. But more importantly, it enables younger generations of Daytona "Beachers" to learn about their city simply and enjoyably.

As the reader travels through the following pages he or she will be taking a magical trip back in time to Daytona Beach at the turn of the Twentieth Century.

The reader will see when visitors went to the ocean and bravely entered the water dressed in heavy woolen bathing suits. The postcard views also take the reader through the decades that followed, when automobiles made jaunts to the ocean more convenient and brought changes that transformed the Central East Coast of Florida. Stay in some of the same hotels, visit the public buildings and walk the same streets. Many of these views afford rare glimpses of first-, second-, or third-generation buildings, some of which no longer exist. By locating remaining structures it is possible to "fill-in" vacant lots or "dematerialize" new structures, thus performing your own urban archeological exploration.

It is hoped that the reader will enjoy this collection of old views of Daytona Beach and will gain an appreciation for what is still here and realize what has been lost. During the mid 1900s many of Daytona Beach's distinctive features were lost forever. Ornamental design became a victim of modernization, cost, and uniformity. What greater homage to our early settlers and developers could we pay than to preserve buildings in remembrance of our beginnings? As we reach for the stars, let us not forget from where we came.

The story begins around 1904, when ocean bathing was still a novelty and picture postcards were new to America, and ends just after World War II. In this half century, the resorts in the Daytona Beach area grew from their small beginnings into busy attractions, and postcards changed, too. Cards from these decades are the most interesting to collectors and casual viewers alike, because they have creatively colored images that speak to our emotions. Most of these cards began as black-and-white photographs and, through the skill of postcard painters, became works of art. Some of the earliest cards were actually hand-painted one by one after printing. These beautiful pieces are now prized as much for their clarity and detail as for their soft, antique palettes. Later cards are brighter, more stylized, and expressively colored in the exuberant style of the 1930s and 1940s. Most postcards manufactured after 1950 are simply reproductions of color photographs.

The author invites you to come and journey back in time to discover a wonderful place!

Nature has bountifully blessed Daytona Beach with an exquisite climate and outdoor activities are pursued year round. Cancelled 1950, $3-5.

Greetings from Daytona Beach, Florida, the world's most famous beach. Circa 1930s, $4-6.

Daytona Beach is located on Florida's northeast coast about ninety miles south of Jacksonville. Circa 1940s, $3-5.

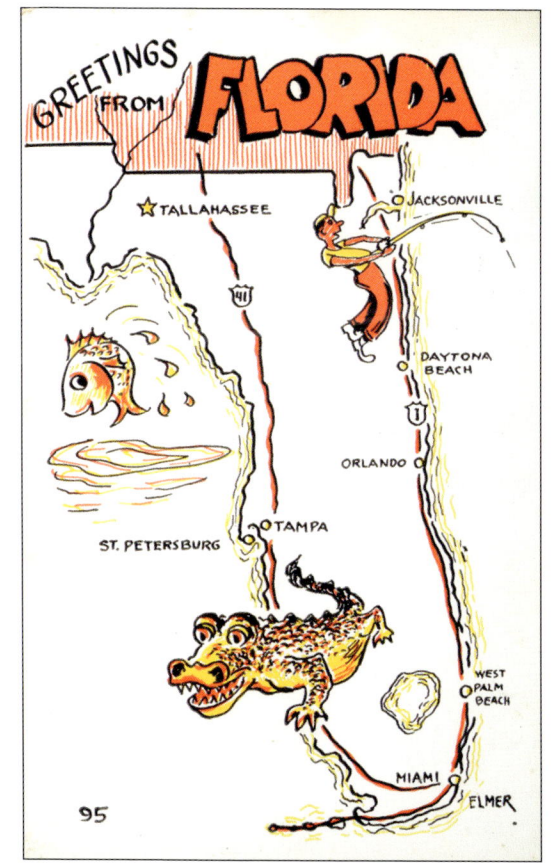

5

Before 1926, the Daytona Beach area was called the Triple Cities. In this year the cities of Daytona, Daytona Beach and Seabreeze were combined to form a resort community with the common name of Daytona Beach. Circa 1930s, $3-5.

Daytona Beach is rich in natural beauty. Subtropical palms, large live oak trees, and flowering shrubs flank the streets. Circa 1940s, $3-5.

Wish You Were Here In Daytona Beach, Florida With Us. Cancelled 1947, $6-8.

Daytona Beach: A Short History

The history of Daytona Beach and its surrounding sister cities began at least 4,000 years ago when aboriginal Indians inhabited this area.

Timucua Indians

The Timucua Indians, descendants of the aboriginal Indians, had several villages in this area when the Spanish arrived in the Sixteenth Century. The Timucua lived throughout much of northeastern Florida, with their territory extending from the east coast to the Ancilla River. Timucua villages were located on the Tomoka River and at Nocoroco (now Tomoka State Park) a few miles north of what is now Daytona Beach. The Spaniards called the Tomoka River "Rio de Timucas" or "River of Timucuas" when they arrived. European explorers and settlers—first the Spaniards, then the French, and later the Spaniards again—conquered and converted many of the Timucua to Christianity. But the Europeans also brought diseases with them that killed off thousands of Indians, diseases against which the Indians had no defense. The few Timucua who were still living in Florida in 1763, when the Spanish gave Florida to the English, left with the Spanish for Cuba. The Timucua did, however, leave clues to their lifestyle through thousands of mounds of shell and debris. Among the more famous mounds in this area are Turtle Mound, Green Mound, Ormond Mound, and Spruce Creek Mound.

English Control of Florida: 1763-1783

Although some Spanish families were given large tracts of land in the present Daytona Beach area, it was not until after 1763, when the British took control, that any serious efforts were made to colonize plantations along the Halifax River.

A wealthy and distinguished Scotsman, Richard Oswald, built the Mount Oswald Plantation in 1766. He was granted 20,000 acres of land along the Halifax and Tomoka rivers, which he planted with rice and indigo. In 1768, Dr. Andrew Turnbull and 1,403 Greek and Minorcan colonists founded New Smyrna and began growing indigo and other crops. Other plantations were also developed.

Second Spanish Occupation: 1783-1821

Florida returned to Spanish control in 1783. The new Spanish government required all settlers to take an oath of allegiance to the Spanish crown or sell their property to Spain. Most settlers elected to leave. Many of the settlers moved to the West Indies. The territory returned to wilderness.

The Spanish offered land grants to Englishmen and Scotsmen on the condition that they plant and cultivate the lands. In the early 1800s, there was a great influx of planters into the Halifax River area and a thriving community prospered from the successful cultivation of cotton, indigo, rice, sugar cane and corn. However, political problems between Spain and America, and domestic violence by criminals and other unsavory characters in the guise of liberating the province from Spanish rule, led to the abandonment of nearly all these plantations.

When Samuel Williams received a Spanish grant of 3,200 acres along the west bank of the Halifax River in 1803, little did he dream that in about a hundred years part of a thriving city called Daytona Beach would be located on his land. Williams named his land the Orange Grove Plantation, built a dwelling house (located near the present corner of South Beach Street and Loomis Avenue) and a sugar mill (located near the corner of Ridgewood and Loomis avenues).

The United States Territorial Period

In the early 1800s it became clear that Spain could no longer maintain her hold on Florida provinces. As a result, in 1821, Florida became a territory of the United States.

At this time, wealthy planters, such as Joseph Woodruff, Charles Bulow, Thomas Dummett, Jose Hernandez, and Orlando Rees, resettled property in this area, imported slaves, and began a sugar cane empire. By 1832 the northeast section of Florida was the center of great activity. Sixteen thriving plantations along the western bank of the Halifax River were producing great quantities of sugar, cotton, indigo, and some rice.

Plantation Era Ends

In 1835-36, the Seminole Indians in Central Florida were angry because the U.S. Government had told them they had to move west of the Mississippi River to make room for white settlers. Many Seminoles, rather than move, decided to stay and fight. Before soldiers stopped them, the Seminoles had burned and pillaged every white owned building they could find. This included the sixteen sugar plantations along the Halifax River. Sugar manufacturing and the grand-scale plantations came to an abrupt end after the devastation of the Second Seminole War. All plantations in this area, including Bulowville, the Orange Grove Plantation, and the Dunlawton Plantation, were completely destroyed. It was reported that all houses south of St. Augustine had been burned to the ground.

Civil War

As the Second Seminole War came to a close, most of the Daytona Beach area was uninhabited and remained so until the end of the Civil War. There were two important activities taking place here during the Civil War, however. Salt works were operated at the Dunlawton Plantation site, while Confederate blockade-runners used Mosquito Inlet (now Ponce de Leon Inlet) to bring goods from the Bahamas Islands.

At the close of the Civil War in March of 1865, Yankees looking for a new location, Southerners looking for new homes as far as possible from the conquerors, and ex-slaves with promises of land streamed into Florida. Port Orange was established in 1861. New Britain began in 1873, but changed its name to Ormond in 1880. Blake (now South Daytona) was platted and named in 1876. Holly Hill's first building was erected in 1877.

Beginning of Daytona

The beginnings of Daytona can be woven around Alfred E. Johnson and James Sawyer. They came in 1867 and purchased 1,071 acres of land, known as the Heriot Tract, from Oliver Swift. Located on the west bank of the Halifax River, it was originally a Spanish grant to Frances Kerr.

In 1871, Matthias Day, an inventor and newspaper publisher from Mansfield, Ohio, purchased a large part of the Samuel Williams grant (Orange Grove Plantation). It was on this grant, and the Frances Kerr grant, that the settlement of Daytona was established.

Among the first large buildings in the area was the Colony House (later named the Palmetto House), designed as a hotel to accommodate settlers until they could build for themselves. Despite the activity and enthusiasm of the pioneers, the town grew slowly because of limited transportation facilities. The first public school was built in 1874 and was also used for public gatherings and as a place of worship. By 1876 there were about twenty-five families living in the community. Daytona developed along two sandy streets—Beach Street running north and south, and Orange Avenue running east and west. Daytona became a municipal corporation on July 26, 1876. The first newspaper to be published in Daytona was the *Halifax Journal* in 1883. At that time there were thirteen stores in Daytona.

Early Transportation

Transportation during the English occupation of Florida was principally by sea from Jacksonville; and by Kings Road, but this highway was neglected and overgrown at the beginning of the United States Territorial Period. In 1876 a stage road was opened west of Daytona to Volusia Landing on the St. Johns River. By 1881 a ferry was established across the Tomoka River, just north of Daytona, connecting with the reconstructed Kings Road into St. Augustine. Five years later the St. Johns and Halifax River Railroad was extended to the Tomoka River. This river, bridged in 1887, permitted the first train to enter Daytona. That same year, the Halifax River was spanned, making the peninsula and ocean beaches more accessible. The railroad brought wealthy tourists from the north to enjoy the sunshine and mild temperatures.

At the dawn of the Twentieth Century there were no streets or highways other than sand trails. The advent of the automobile resulted in improved roads throughout Volusia County. By 1910, hard surface roads connected Daytona with DeLand and New Smyrna. The roads were popular driveways with automobilists, horse lovers and the bicyclist.

Railroad Brings Tourists to Daytona

Henry M. Flagler, a railroad and hotel tycoon, who played an important part in the development of the East Coast of Florida, extended his railroad south from St. Augustine, and in 1890 he purchased the Ormond Hotel, a large resort hotel at Ormond. Daytona sprang to life with the influx of winter visitors and soon had a population of 2,000. Although developed almost solely as a resort, the area was the center of a prosperous citrus industry. The area was also involved in producing turpentine, cutting trees for lumber and growing papaya and preparing products made from this melon-like fruit. By the early 1900s, northern-based millionaires were wintering in Daytona, living three months of the year in hotels in the downtown Daytona area.

Charles Burgoyne, a wealthy publisher from New York, built a home and casino on Beach Street in downtown Daytona and is credited with the earliest promotion of tourism in the area. Daytona became a city of fine homes and was noted for beautiful drives. By 1910, the city had electric lights, an ice plant, a weekly paper (*Daytona Gazette*), social clubs, a yacht club, an automobile club, good stores and one bank.

Racing on the Beach

The early 1900s brought the automobile to the Daytona area. In 1902 the beach was enjoyed at a leisurely pace during horse and buggy days. Then along came the horseless carriage, well ahead of decent highways. Men with their new machines realized that the hard packed sandy beach was a natural for automotive time trials. Some of the more daring began racing their automobiles along the beach.

Wealthy automobile manufacturers brought with them their early models by barge and ox team to their winter home, the Ormond Hotel. At the Ormond Garage, up the street from the hotel, they talked shop, shined up their buggies, tuned up their autos, and from this original "Gasoline Alley" garage, they wheeled their cars to the hard-packed sand beach to test them for speed.

In 1903 the Florida East Coast Automobile Association was formed to promote beach racing. Over the next three decades many speed tests were conducted on the beach racecourse. Famous names that were involved with beach racing include Ransom E. Olds, Alexander Winton, John Jacob Astor, William K. Vanderbilt, Rollin White, Henry Ford, Jimmy Murphy, L. Malford Dusenberg, Ralph DePalma, Barney Oldfield, Frank Lockhart, Lee Bible, Henry Segrave and Sir Malcolm Campbell. Beach racing put Daytona Beach on the map. Sir Malcolm Campbell's official speed record of 276.82 mph was established in 1935 while driving his *Bluebird V* racing car on the beach course. This record-breaking run marked the limit of speed racing on the Ormond-Daytona Beach racecourse.

Triple Cities Become One

Until 1926 the city of Daytona occupied only the west shore of the Halifax River. Across the river lay Seabreeze and Daytona Beach, separate municipalities. During the boom period of 1924-26, Daytona and the small community of Port Orange began wrangling over the annexation of the peninsula south of Daytona Beach. Landowners in the disputed territory demanded that they be included in Daytona. This was done in 1924, and the Daytona borders were extended to the southern end of the peninsula. Two years later Seabreeze and Daytona Beach voted for annexation and the three cities, with a single municipal government, were united under the name Daytona Beach. Daytona Beach became known as the city with a triple waterfront, one on the Atlantic Ocean and one on each side of the Halifax River.

The Daytona Beach Chamber of Commerce immediately started advertising the "new" city, pointing out that yachting, motor boating, canoeing, golf, surf bathing, fishing, hunting, and many other activities were popular in this area.

In 1929 the Daytona Beach Boardwalk opened, however, Florida's economy—and lure as a popular vacation destination—dropped considerably when the stock market crashed the same year. It wasn't until the late 1930s when the Bandshell, Clock Tower, and other amenities were completed that the Daytona Beach area again took its place in the sun.

Bill France and a group of automobile enthusiasts established the National Association of Stock Car Auto Racing (NASCAR) in 1947 to add some structure to automobile racing. In 1959, Mr. France built the Daytona International Speedway, which has turned into a very large motor sport complex, hosting many annual races, including the Daytona 500. What began as a rich man's thrill ride evolved into the sport that gave Daytona Beach its international reputation as the center of stock car racing's universe.

Modern Daytona Beach

Today, the Daytona Beach area entertains more than eight million visitors each year. Visitors come from around the world to relax on one of the most beautiful beaches in Florida.

Like many popular locations, the Daytona Beach area is comprised of a number of cities and communities. Centrally located Daytona Beach is surrounded by seven smaller cities: Daytona Beach Shores, Holly Hill, Ormond Beach, Ormond-By-The-Sea, Ponce Inlet, Port Orange, and South Daytona. Within this tightly knit enclave of communities, one finds that each has its own unique character and appeal.

Chapter One
Changing Streets and Byways

When roads were first developed in Daytona, bicycles were a popular form of transportation. This hand-colored postcard shows bicyclists cruising along Beach Street. Bicycles may have been popular, however, automobiles were not. In 1897, Charles G. Burgoyne, one of Daytona's most progressive mayors, recommended that City Council refuse to license motor vehicles. However, it is interesting to note that Commodore Burgoyne later owned the second automobile in Daytona. Copyright 1904, $3-5.

An early Beach Street scene showing the home of Charles Grover Burgoyne, the premier showplace home of Daytona. Burgoyne, a lavish distributor of his income, liberally contributed to municipal improvements in the City of Daytona—paving the streets, street lighting, seawall, and esplanade along Beach Street. He passed away in this home in 1916 and is buried in Pinewood Cemetery, Circa 1900s, $2-4.

A busy Beach Street: it was here that most of Daytona's businesses were located. Cancelled 1910, $5-7.

10570. BUSINESS SECTION OF BEACH STREET, DAYTONA, FLA.

Daytona, Fla. Beach Street.

Shown are three horse-drawn carriages and a lonely bicycle on Beach Street. Circa 1907, $6-8.

This postcard shows the post office, located at the corner of Magnolia Avenue and Beach Street, in the center of Daytona's business district. The card also illustrates the three most popular types of transportation: the bicycle, the horse-and-buggy, and the automobile. Circa 1910, $6-8.

Daytona, Florida. Post Office and Beach Street.

The view is from looking north on Beach Street. Traffic on the street included automobiles, bicycles, and horse-drawn carriages. Circa 1909, $7-9.

13

GLIMPSE OF THE ESPLANADE, SOUTH FROM CASINO, DAYTONA, FLA.

The Merchants Bank building, shown on the right side, was built on Beach Street in 1910, with additions made in 1926. It has several unusual features, including ionic capitals flanked by rams' heads and stained-glass ceiling skylights in the main room. The structure, which is now occupied by the Halifax Historical Museum, is a fine example of Beaux Arts Classicism. Circa 1920s, $2-4.

The fruits of mass production: rural America took to the car very early. This is Beach Street, the main street in Daytona, where virtually every car in sight is a Model T Ford. By 1920 there were some nine million cars on American roads and every second car coming off the production lines was a Tin Lizzie. Cancelled 1926, $2-4.

Beach Street and River Front, Daytona Beach, Florida.

Magnolia Avenue looking east from Ridgewood Avenue. In the early 1900s this avenue contained modern residences and large hotels, all among magnificent oaks and palmettos. Circa 1907, $6-8.

Looking north on South Beach Street in Daytona, the Halifax River Yacht Club is shown on the distant right. It was founded in 1896 and had a membership of one hundred nine in 1903. Cancelled 1913, $4-6.

A Magnolia Avenue scene in downtown Daytona is illustrated in this Alligator Border postcard. The Alligator Border Series, published by Langsdorf, is in great demand with postcard collectors. Cancelled 1910, $40-45.

Daytona, Florida.
Bay Street, East.

In 1900 there were no automobiles in Volusia County. A year later, two or three cars appeared in Daytona, but automobiles were still a novelty in 1915. It was an occasion worthy of a postcard when one was seen on this dirt road (Bay Street, East) in Daytona. Circa 1910, $3-5.

BAY STREET, LOOKING WEST, DAYTONA, FLA.

"How is little Philadelphia? Not nearly as quiet and peaceful as this I'll bet a donut," is the message on a card showing Bay Street, looking west. The first home on the right was named "La Vergne Mansion." Cancelled 1919, $1-3.

Cedar Avenue and Hotel, Daytona, Fla

This view shows a lonely automobile traveling on Cedar Avenue (now Cedar Street). Cancelled 1910, $4-6.

A view of Cedar Avenue (now Cedar Street) looking east. The sender of this card, mailed at Daytona on March 7, wrote, "We sailed up the Tomoka River where alligators are lying on the river banks and we touched them with poles as we sailed along. Tomorrow we are going to visit the largest orange grove in Florida." Cancelled 1911, $2-4.

This postcard, mailed at Daytona on February 18, shows that Orange Avenue had little traffic problems. Cancelled 1908, $3-5.

Daytona, Fla. Orange Avenue.

Volusia Avenue (now International Speedway Boulevard) was the main east-west cross-town thoroughfare in Daytona. Cancelled 1910, $3-5.

Looking south on Ridgewood Avenue from Magnolia Avenue, the only vehicle on the road was a horse-drawn carriage. Cancelled 1913, $2-4.

Looking north on Ridgewood Avenue, the Ridgewood Hotel is shown on the left. This postcard shows a beautiful tree-lined road that connected Daytona with New Smyrna (South) and Ormond Beach (North). Cancelled 1909, $2-4.

Like birds migrating south for the winter, tourists from the north motored to Florida, taking the Dixie Highway to Daytona. The sender of this postcard of Ridgewood Avenue wrote, "The timber is beautiful large live oaks hanging with the beautiful grey moss (Spanish moss). Lots of pines and palm trees of many different kinds. The ferns are beautiful—acres of them waist high." Cancelled 1913, $4-6.

Looking north from Seabreeze Avenue (now Main Street), this sand path was the beginning of Ocean Avenue. The 74-room Seaside Inn is shown in the foreground on the left. Circa 1905, $8-10.

These automobiles are driving south on Ocean Avenue in front of the Daytona Beach Hotel. In the early 1900s, the Daytona Beach area had miles and miles of good roads and a wide, hard-sand beach that made motoring a pleasure every day of the year. Circa 1910, $10-12.

Ocean Boulevard, Daytona Beach, Florida, Showing Daytona Beach Hotel.

"Hello Rudolph. Did you see this place when you were in Daytona Beach? Send me some cards and I will send you some," was written on the back of this card of Ocean Avenue. Cancelled 1920, $8-10.

Daytona Beach, Fla. Seabreeze Ave.

Looking west on Seabreeze Avenue (now Main Street) shown are horse-drawn carriages, early automobiles, the Van Valzah Hotel (on the left) and the Seaside Inn (on the right). Cancelled 1911, $8-10.

Daytona Beach, Florida, The Van Valzah and Dancing Pavilion in Distance.

Looking east on Seabreeze Avenue (now Main Street), the Seaside Inn is shown on the north side of the street. The Pier, Dancing Pavilion and Van Valzah Hotel are shown on the south side of the street. Circa 1910, $10-12.

Sea Breeze Ave., Daytona Beach, Fla.

The sender of this card of Seabreeze Avenue (now Main Street), mailed at Ormond on February 11, wrote, "This view is of a town five miles south of where I spent a very pleasant last evening." Cancelled 1912, $7-9.

Looking west on Main Street, the Van Valzah Hotel is shown on the south side of the street and the Seaside Inn is shown in the foreground on the north side of the street. Circa 1926, $3-5.

Main Street, Daytona Beach, Fla.

Bicycle riders on Ocean Boulevard (now Seabreeze Boulevard) in Seabreeze. Cancelled 1905, $3-5.

Ocean Boulevard, Sea Breeze, Fla.

with greetings of os.m.

Looking east on Seabreeze's Ocean Boulevard (now Seabreeze Boulevard), the Clarendon Hotel is shown in the background. This hotel was nationally famous as the hotel you drove under to get to the beach. In the early 1900s the town of Seabreeze was a winter resort for the wealthy. After spring in those days, you could shoot a cannon down Ocean Boulevard and hit no one. Everyone had gone north to his or her summer homes. Cancelled 1911, $3-5.

Clarendon Inn, near Daytona, Fla.

Feb. 1st. 1911.

584.

Chapter Two
Community Life

The Burgoyne Place,
Daytona, Fla.

DAYTONA, Florida
C C.
Burgoyne Residence.

The Burgoyne mansion was the center for social functions in the late 1890s and early 1900s. The house was demolished in 1941 to make way for a shopping center. Cancelled 1909, $5-7.

In 1896, Charles Grover Burgoyne built a castle-like mansion on North Beach Street between Volusia Avenue (now International Speedway Boulevard) and Bay Street. Burgoyne became one of the city's outstanding benefactors and was active in all aspects of community life in Daytona. The mansion, which was sometimes called the Burgoyne Castle, was surrounded with other buildings. Cancelled 1912, $5-7.

The Country Club. Cancelled 1908, $6-8.

This postcard shows the sugar cane grinding mill from the Samuel Williams Plantation, the plantation on which the city of Daytona Beach is located. The crude mill was located at the corner of Ridgewood and Loomis avenues. The mill, which was used to press sugar cane, was relocated to Sugar Mill Botanical Gardens in Port Orange in 1965. Circa 1907, $10-12.

In 1911, Charles Grover Burgoyne, an ardent music fan, inaugurated free winter band concerts in Daytona on Beach Street. Every afternoon and evening the band was heard in the park. Cancelled 1914, $15-17.

City Hall and South Bridge, Daytona, Fla.

Scene around the Band Stand. Cancelled 1914, $16-18.

Watching the Saracina Royal Italian
Band perform in downtown Daytona.
These annual winter concerts were
popular with both residents and visitors.
Circa 1910, $6-8.

Band Stand, Daytona, Fla.

THE CASINO, DAYTONA, FLA.

1252 CASINO BURGOYNE, DAYTONA, FLORIDA.

In the early 1910s, Charles Grover Burgoyne launched a beautification project for Beach Street when he built the Esplanada, a cement walkway extending from Orange Avenue to Bay Street, bordered by beautiful light poles bought from the City of Buffalo, New York. The Burgoyne Casino and a coquina rock seawall were built about the same time. Circa 1910s, $6-8.

Charles Grover Burgoyne built the Burgoyne Casino in 1915 on the corner of Beach Street and Orange Avenue for a free public entertainment center. This structure, which he gave to the city, was used as an auditorium. It was a principal gathering place that housed indoor recreation with shuffleboard and bowling. The Casino burned to the ground in 1937. Circa 1920s, $6-8.

AIRPLANE VIEW OF CASINO AND BEACH ST., DAYTONA, FLA.

This bird's eye view of Beach Street shows a riverside view of the Burgoyne Casino, Circa 1920s, $2-4.

Winter visitors playing lawn bowling at the Burgoyne Casino.
Circa 1920s, $1-3.

The S. Cornelia Young Memorial Library has operated from its present address since 1916 when Captain Charles A. Young, a clipper ship captain from Connecticut, donated the building in honor of his wife Sarah Cornelia Young. The original building was modified in 1931 and again in 1961. The library is on the National Registry of Historic Buildings.
Circa 1910s, $2-4.

Orange Avenue Bridge with the Daytona Library on the left and the city jail on the right. The attractive two-room, gray cement block building, the area's first library building, was on City Island, just north of South Bridge. Books for the library were cataloged in 1910. In 1920, when Daytona built a new City Hall, the Daytona Public Library, with its 4,000 volumes, was moved to the second floor of the City Hall building, where it remained until the mid 1940s.
Circa 1910s, $6-8.

The first Palmetto Club was built on Orange Avenue in 1903. Elegant oak, magnolia and palm trees surrounded the clubhouse, which was owned by the large and popular Woman's Club. Circa 1907, $2-4.

In 1911 the first Elks Club was built on the corner of Volusia (now International Speedway Boulevard) and Palmetto avenues. The club was demolished in the 1960s to make way for the widening of Volusia Avenue. Circa 1913, $2-4.

The Second Palmetto Club, a Spanish style Mediterranean Revival building, was built in the mid 1910s. It was the first building in Daytona to be completely lit by electricity. A fire destroyed the clubhouse in 1971 and a new Palmetto Club was built on South Beach Street in 1972. Cancelled 1917, $3-5.

The Peninsula Club, organized in 1908 and federated in 1914, built a clubhouse in 1922 at Goodall Avenue and South Peninsula Drive. Circa 1920s, $1-3.

Casino, Chamber of Commerce and Recreation Headquarters, Daytona Beach, Fla.

Daytona Beach's recreation headquarters was located on City Island between the city proper and the beach. Cancelled 1941, $1-3.

Brownie was a stray that took up residence at the corner of Orange Avenue and Beach Street in Daytona Beach. Taxi-cab drivers furnished him with a doghouse, fed him, and helped finance his upkeep by selling postcards, such as the one shown here. The story of Brownie was printed in national magazines and newspapers, and he even received Christmas cards and presents from people throughout America. Brownie died of old age in 1954 and the City of Daytona Beach provided him a final resting place in Riverfront Park. Circa 1940s, $18-20.

SEABREEZE, FLA. PRIVATE GROUNDS NEAR THE COLONADES.

This postcard shows the grounds and home of C. C. and Helen Wilmans Post, which was built by S. H. Gove and was said to be one of the finest residences in the state south of St. Augustine. It later became the Bellevue-Halifax Hotel and was demolished in 1959. It was common for the homes of prominent local residents to appear on postcards. Cancelled 1911, $8-10.

Daytona, Fla., in January.
Rose Garden at Winter Home of
Benjamin L. Armstrong.

Elizabeth Armstrong, the sender of this postcard, wrote: "This is where Angela used to live in Daytona, before we moved over to St. Petersburg. Our cottage is the one on the corner with a round piazza and Angela's grandfather's cottage is just beyond. These are rose bushes in the front yard." Cancelled 1924, $2-4.

Bungalows, Daytona, Florida.

These three bungalows, located at the northeast corner of South Street and Ridgewood Avenue, are listed on the National Register of Historic Places. Circa 1914, $1-3.

Chapter Three
Hotels

HOTEL ADIRONDACK, DAYTONA, FLA.   "PRETTIEST RESORT IN THE WORLD."   SPERRY & CUNNINGHAM, PROPS.

The Adirondack Hotel was on Beach Street in downtown Daytona. Circa 1915, $3-5.

The Austin Hotel, located on the southwest corner of North Beach Street and Third Avenue, was one of Daytona's landmark hotels since the beginning of the twentieth century. The hotel was razed in 1935 to make room for a Firestone Auto Supply and Service Station. The location was later occupied by the Daytona Beach Federal Savings and Loan, and is now the Child Care Resource Network. Cancelled 1915, $1-3.

In 1923, Julian Arroyo, a political refugee from Venezuela and law partner of Franklin Delano Roosevelt, built a 124-room apartment complex called Arroyo Gardens at 400 South Ridgewood Avenue. The Spanish-Moorish designed complex had tiled patios, detailed terra cotta trim, swimming pool and lush landscaping. In 1940 the hotel became the Daytona Terrace Hotel. In 1942, Ransom Olds, of early automobile fame, purchased the hotel to fulfill his dream of creating a retirement home for ministers and missionaries. He named the facility Olds Hall. Cancelled 1925, $1-3.

ARROYO GARDENS ON RIDGEWOOD AVE., DAYTONA, FLA.

The three-story Breakers Hotel, next to the Daytona Beach Hotel on the Ocean Avenue block south of Main Street, was built in 1914 and destroyed by fire in 1946. Cancelled 1920, $3-5.

The Barbe Hotel, located at 120 South Ocean Avenue, was a year-round hotel located directly on the oceanfront. It was heated by hot water in the winter and cooled by ocean breezes in the summer. It was razed to provide a parking lot. Circa 1920s, $7-9.

The Carter Hall Hotel, at 440 South Ridgewood Avenue, had rooms with automatic steam heat and private baths for reasonable rates. Circa 1920s, $1-3.

The Clarendon Hotel in Seabreeze (now Daytona Beach) as it appeared in 1899. Various fires caused the appearance of this historically significant hotel to change several times over the years. It burned in 1909. Circa 1908, $5-7.

The Bellevue-Halifax Hotel, located at Ocean Boulevard (now Seabreeze Boulevard) and Halifax Avenue, was a Daytona Beach Guest House. Originally, it was the home of C. C. and Helen Wilmans Post, who platted the town of Seabreeze (now part of Daytona Beach). It was demolished in 1959. Cancelled 1938, $3-5.

This view shows the Clarendon Hotel, located at the beach end of Ocean Boulevard (now Seabreeze Boulevard) in Seabreeze (now Daytona Beach), with its bridge over the beach approach. The building burned down in 1909 and was rebuilt in 1911. In the early part of the twentieth century, the Seabreeze district was a winter resort for the wealthy. Mrs. C. C. Post, better known as Helen Wilmans Post, personally planned and supervised the sixty-foot wide boulevard pictured in this postcard. Circa 1907, $6-8.

Seabreeze, Fla. Ocean Boulevard showing The Clarendon

The Clarendon Inn, Sea Breeze, Fla.

In 1945 the Clarendon Hotel was open during the winter months from January to May. Cancelled 1915, $4-6.

An airplane view of the Clarendon Hotel in Seabreeze. Circa 1920s, $3-5.

In 1896, to accommodate tourists and prospective land purchasers, local developers C. C. Post and Charles A. Ballough built the 120-room Colonnades Hotel on the southeast corner of Halifax Avenue and Ocean Boulevard (now Seabreeze Boulevard). In 1901 it was advertised as "a modern hotel, with electric lights, steam heat and private baths." The hotel burned down in 1909. Copyright 1904, $6-8.

In 1945 the Clarendon Hotel became the Sheraton Plaza Hotel and later the Daytona Plaza Hotel, the Howard Johnson Plaza, the Holiday Inn Sunsplash, and is now the Plaza Resort & Spa. Cancelled 1937, $2-4.

Built on the beach in 1908, the 60-room Daytona Beach Hotel was located on Ocean Avenue next to the Breakers Hotel and near the Seaside Inn. Cancelled 1909, $3-5.

The Daytona Terrace was located on U.S. Highway 1 in downtown Daytona Beach. Circa 1930s, $3-5.

The Daytona Plaza Hotel at the eastern end of Seabreeze Boulevard was previously the Clarendon and Sheraton Plaza hotels. Circa 1950s, $1-3.

Leon Despland built the Despland Hotel, at the southeast corner of Palmetto and Magnolia avenues, in 1901. By 1912 it had been expanded to accommodate up to two hundred guests. In 1917 the hotel was bought by T.F. Williams who renamed it the Williams Hotel. It was demolished in the late 1960s. Cancelled 1907, $3-5.

Hotel Des Pland, DAYTONA, Fla.   Cor. Magnolia ave + Palmetto St.   3198.

The El Cortez-Manor located at Seabreeze Boulevard and North Atlantic Avenue was previously the El Cortez Hotel and later, Seabreeze Manor. Circa 1930s, $1-3.

The thirty-room Gables Hotel was located on Volusia Avenue (now International Speedway Boulevard) between Palmetto Avenue and Beach Street. The Greyhound Bus Station was located to the left and Pep's Cafe and Soda Shop was located to the right. The structure was demolished in 1967. Circa 1920s, $3-5.

Not all of the city's lodging was on a grand scale: numerous small hotels and boarding houses dotted the area. One of these was the Fernwood Hotel, on the northwest corner of Wild Olive Avenue and Main Street. The hotel closed for several years; in 2001, it was demolished. Circa 1920s, $1-3.

THE GENEVA, SEABREEZE-DAYTONA BEACH, FLORIDA

The Hamilton, Daytona, Fla.

GRAND ATLANTIC HOTEL, DAYTONA, FLA.

The Geneva Hotel, built in 1911, was on Ocean Boulevard (now Seabreeze Boulevard) midway between the Halifax River and the beach. Circa 1930s, $1-3.

The 20-room Hotel Hamilton, located at 214 South Palmetto Avenue, was only one block from Daytona's main business district and theaters. In 1912, its rates were $2.50 per day and upward. Circa 1910s, $3-5.

The Grand Atlantic Hotel, on the northwest corner of North Beach Street and Third Avenue, was built in the early 1880s. This popular downtown 125-room hotel later became known as the Ocean View, Holly Inn and, around 1908, it was the Prince George Hotel. In the 1950s, a Sears, Roebuck & Co. store was built on this site. It is now the Volusia County Administration Center, Circa 1904, $8-10.

The Lyndhurst Hotel was on south Ridgewood Avenue; in 1952, weekly rates were $7 to $10. Circa 1910, $3-5.

The Morgan Hotel, was on the southeast corner of Volusia (now International Speedway Boulevard) and Palmetto avenues, where the S & S Cafeteria was located for many years. Rates at the Morgan Hotel started at $2.50 per night. Circa 1930s, $3-5.

The 80-room Oaks Hotel, on the west side of Ridgewood Avenue between Bay Street and Third Avenue, was open during the season, December to May. They advertised that New England cooks prepared meals for the guests. Circa 1907, $6-8.

A bird's eye view of the Ocean Park Hotel on Ocean Avenue. Also shown are the Clock Tower, the Boardwalk, the Main Street Pier and Casino, the beach and ocean. This hotel, and adjoining houses on Ocean Avenue, were demolished to make room for the 437-room Marriott Hotel (became the Adam's Mark Hotel Resort in 1995 and later a Hilton Hotel). Cancelled 1942, $4-6.

PARTIAL VIEW OF THE OSCEOLA-GRAMATAN, "A DISTINCTIVE HOTEL", DAYTONA, FLA.

The Oleander Inn was located at 531 North Grandview Avenue. It had forty rooms, thirty baths, and was remodeled in 1937. Cancelled 1952, $1-3.

The Osceola-Gramatan Hotel, at 1130 S. Ridgewood Avenue, with its twenty-four cottages, could accommodate 300 guests. Circa 1920s, $1-3.

Palmetto House, Daytona, Fla., C. O. Chamberlin, Pro.

Published in Germany for G. W. Morris, Portland, Maine.

In 1870, Matthias Day came to this area, purchased property and began platting his proposed town of Daytona. In 1871 he built the Colony House at the corner of South Beach Street and Loomis Avenue to accommodate the early settlers until they could build their own homes. It was later called the Palmetto House, as shown in the postcard, because it originally had a temporary palmetto-thatched roof. In 1901, the Palmetto House charged $2 to $3 a day and was open from November 15 to May 1. Like many of the early hotels, it was destroyed by fire in 1922. The New Colony House Condominium is now located on this site. A historical marker mounted on a coquina rock foundation marks this historic location. Circa 1905, $7-9.

PIER HOTEL . . . Daytona Beach, Florida

The Port Orange House, located on the northwest corner of Halifax Drive and Dunlawton Avenue, was built in 1872. It later became a tuberculosis sanitarium, Alligator Inn, Riverside Hotel, and finally, Riverside Apartments. The structure was demolished in 1997. Circa 1907, $7-9.

The Pier Hotel, located at the southeast corner of Ocean Avenue and Main Street, was diagonally across from the much larger Seaside Inn. This building had been the home to a variety of businesses until it was recently demolished. Circa 1930s, $4-6.

The Prince George Hotel was located on the west bank of Halifax River in downtown Daytona. It was formerly the Grand Atlantic Hotel, the Ocean View Hotel, and Holly Inn Hotel. Circa 1908, $5-7.

Daytona, Fla.   Prince George Hotel.

Princess Issena, Sea Breeze, Fla.

The Princess Issena Hotel on Ocean Boulevard (now Seabreeze Boulevard). This postcard shows the twenty-seven room hotel as it looked in 1908 when Mr. and Mrs. C. C. Post opened the facility. Circa 1908, $13-15.

Princess Issena, Seabreeze, Fla.—62

This postcard shows the Princess Issena after many additions were made, including an inn, cottages, apartments, theater, large restaurant and swimming pool. The beautiful hotel rested in a tropical setting of an entire landscaped city block. The hotel became the property of the Sheraton Corporation in the 1940s, and twenty years later, it became a retirement home for senior citizens. It was demolished in 1981 and the property remained vacant for many years. Today First Union Bank occupies part of the location. Circa 1920s, $3-5.

The Ridgewood Hotel was located on Ridgewood Avenue between Magnolia and Orange avenues. Erected by Dr. James Rose in 1894, the hotel hosted a number of important guests, including English race drivers Sir Malcolm Campbell and Sir Henry Segrave. Many guests stayed at the hotel while attending early automobile races on the beach. Shown here is an early version of the hotel. Circa 1904, $3-5.

8141. HOTEL RIDGEWOOD, DAYTONA, FLA.

COPYRIGHT, 1904, BY DETROIT PHOTOGRAPHIC CO.

Daytona, Florida. The Prospect—View from the Ridgewood.

The 22-room Prospect Guest Hotel was located on the east side of South Ridgewood Avenue, opposite the Ridgewood Hotel. The hotel was convenient to the railroad station, the post office, and the Daytona business district. Circa 1910s, $4-6.

D-102 RIDGEWOOD HOTEL — DAYTONA BEACH, FLA.

U.S. 1

7A-H2470

A view of the Ridgewood Hotel after a coquina face-lift was made to the front in 1912. In the mid 1970s, many large oak trees in front of the hotel were removed when U.S. Highway 1 was widened. In 1975, the hotel was demolished. Later, Commercial Bank at Daytona Beach was built on the site. Circa 1910s, $1-3.

Feb. 14- '08

SCHMIDT'S VILLA, DAYTONA, FLA. *Spent 2 days here. um "truck" on plan. Royally entertained at winter + round of B.R. Sums altsday. to P. Beach & Miami to-day. Weather dili gint... ...yours, J. D. McKinney—*

HOTEL SEABREEZE, DAYTONA BEACH, FLORIDA.

"Why don't some of you all write?" was an often-penned postcard message in the days before telephones became common. This card, mailed in 1912, shows Schmidt's Villa, located on the northwest corner of Second Avenue (now Dr. Mary McLeod Bethune Boulevard) and North Beach Street, a downtown Daytona hotel that had accommodations for one hundred tourists. Cancelled 1908, $3-5.

The Seabreeze Hotel was located on the oceanfront. Cancelled 1926, $6-8.

The Seaside Inn, located at the northwest corner of Seabreeze (now Main Street) and Ocean avenues, opened in 1890 in Goodall (became Daytona Beach in 1905). The hotel had verandas that overlooked the beach and ocean. It was a first class hotel that was popular with winter visitors. Circa 1905, $5-7.

Daytona Beach, Fla. Seaside Inn.

THE SHERATON PLAZA, DAYTONA BEACH, FLORIDA

The Sheraton Plaza Hotel was previously the Clarendon Hotel; it changed ownership several times and is now a condominium facility. Circa 1940s, $3-5.

On December 14, 1947, Bill France, Sr. brought together a group of racing enthusiasts in an effort to add some structure to auto racing. The group met at the Streamline Hotel, and conceived a national sanctioning body called the National Association for Stock Car Auto Racing (NASCAR). Circa 1950s, $4-6.

The sixty-room, three-story Val Valzah Hotel, on the south side of Seabreeze Avenue (now Main Street) in Daytona Beach, was located a short walk from the beach. Circa 1910, $8-10.

The Hotel Troy, located at the corner of Volusia (now International Speedway Boulevard) and Palmetto avenues, was built in 1885. Originally opened by William and Mary Troy as the "Troy House," it was popular with winter guests from November until May. Circa 1953, $1-3.

This small Whitehall Hotel at 640 North Atlantic Avenue later became the eleven-story Whitehall Inn with 293 ocean-view rooms. Circa 1930s, $8-10.

The Windsor Hotel was located on South Beach Street in downtown Daytona and was demolished in the 1940s; an apartment building now occupies the site. Circa 1930s, $2-4.

The Williams Hotel was located on the corner of Magnolia and Palmetto avenues. Winter rates were $3.50 per night. Circa 1920s, $3-5.

Chapter Four
The Beach

COPR. DETROIT PHOTOGRAPHIC CO

8143   BEACH AT SEABREEZE, FLA.

Horses, carriages and beach strollers on the beach at Seabreeze (now part of Daytona Beach). This 1904 postcard illustrates the popularity of the beach. The ladies and their long dresses are certainly a contrast to today's bikini clad sun worshippers.
Circa 1907, $10-12.

This postcard shows the Silver Sands of Daytona Beach. Beach vehicles include horse-drawn carriages, riding horses, and a bicycle. Circa 1904, $5-7.

Low Tide at Daytona Beach, Florida

Sand sailing on the beach in the 1890s. Daytona Beach has always been a party beach, Florida's version of Coney Island. Up until the early 1900s, these sailing vehicles could be rented at beachside hotels. Circa 1905, $3-5.

DAYTONA BEACH, FLA.

SURF BATHING, DAYTONA, BEACH, FLA.

Northern tourists who could afford a winter vacation in sunny Daytona Beach liked to brag to their friends back home about the delightful climate here. And this postcard was a dandy way to do it. It shows a "Bathing Scene" at Daytona Beach. Circa 1907, $5-7.

Swimming was a favorite activity for residents and visitors alike. This view reveals what the well-dressed swimmer wore in Daytona Beach. Cancelled 1911, $6-8.

One doesn't see many hand-painted bathing scenes like this anymore! Cancelled 1909, $10-12.

THE BATHING IS SUPERB AND THE BATHING GIRLS DIVINE.
Greetings from Daytona Beach, Fla.

Whales on beach, near New Smyrna, Fla.

A school of nine young Sperm Whales mysteriously came ashore on New Smyrna Beach just south of Daytona Beach. Four were alive for several hours after they were found. Cancelled 1909, $8-10.

Ready for a Swim, Daytona Beach, Fla. 1917

Winter bathing at Daytona Beach. This city has, for many years, been a favorite resort for visitors from throughout the country. Surf bathing was always a popular pastime, even when the bather was almost fully dressed. Cancelled 1917, $10-12.

Watching the Bathers.

DAYTONA BEACH, FLA.

One of the greatest assets of Daytona Beach has always been its beautiful Atlantic Ocean coastline. Early visitors enjoyed the sandy beach and ocean water. Hundreds of bathers splashed together in the waves, while hundreds more watched them from the shore. Cancelled 1911, $10-12.

This beach scene shows the Florida East Coast Automobile Club on the left. Cancelled 1915, $4-6.

Daytona Beach and Florida East Coast Automobile Club, Daytona Beach, Fla.

Aeroplane on the Beach, Daytona, Fla.—21

An airplane landing on the beach. In the early 1900s, the City of Daytona Beach passed a law that no airplanes could land within the city limits except on the beach. Then, in the late 1930s, a law was passed stating airplanes could not use the beach for landings and takeoffs. This law is still in effect today. Circa 1920s, $12-14.

Clarendon Hotel from the Beach, Seabreeze, Fla.

The first aviation event occurred on the beach when Israel Ludlow, a New York lawyer, sent a glider to Ormond Beach as an added attraction during the 1906 auto beach races. Up to the 1930s, airplanes landed and took off from the beach. Shown is a biplane on the beach side of the Clarendon Hotel in Seabreeze (now Daytona Beach). Circa 1920s, $12-14.

Daytona Beach, Florida.—39

One would almost think this beach scene was the Daytona Beach airport—one airplane in the sky and two airplanes on the sandy beach. Barnstormers, mostly World War I veterans who had trained on the beach at Daytona, returned after the war and used the beach just north of the Main Street Pier as a landing field in 1919 and the early 1920s. Cancelled 1922, $12-14.

In the early 1900s, people began to realize that the beach would make a good airstrip. The beach was 300 to 500 feet wide at low tide. And it ran in a straight line for almost twenty-five miles. Pilots landed on the beach and parked their airplanes up close to the sand dunes. Shown are two biplanes parked behind the Clarendon Hotel in Seabreeze (now Daytona Beach). Captain J.O. Jorstad would take tourists on short airplane rides. Circa 1920, $12-14.

BLUE BIRD PASSENGER FLIGHTS CAPT. JORSTAD

9844

Clarenden Hotel, Daytona, Fla.

D-26 WINTER BATHING AT DAYTONA BEACH, FLA.

94176

Like ants at a picnic, people and their automobiles packed the beaches at Daytona Beach. Cancelled 1924, $6-8.

The Finest Beach in the World, Daytona, Fla.—25
De Palma's World Record Made Here.

All over the world, the beach was very much the place to be in the 1920s. Cancelled 1922, $6-8.

Beach, Fla.

The original Main Street Pier was built by Thomas H. Keating. It was 600 feet long and built of palmetto logs. The original casino was located on the southeast corner of Main Street and Ocean Avenue. The Pier and Casino became the social hub of the entire area. Transportation was by horse and buggy or bicycle. Cancelled 1912, $10-12.

Pavilion, Daytona, Florida.

This postcard, mailed at Daytona on November 13, shows the Keating Pier and Pavilion (Casino). It was built in 1900, burned in 1919, and replaced with the current Main Street Pier and Casino in 1925. Cancelled 1914, $10-12.

Seabreeze, Fla, The Pier.

The Clarendon Hotel Pier. The sender of this card wrote, "This is where I went this morning to see the sharks. This pier is only a few steps from my room." Cancelled 1906, $8-10.

Daytona Beach, Fla. Surf Bathing.

A popular activity for Daytona Beach visitors was frolicking at the seashore. The sender of this card, postmarked at Daytona Beach on February 5, wrote, "We are enjoying this beach very much. It is the finest beach I have ever seen." This view shows the end of the Keating Pier and the bathing dress of the day. It cost ten cents to walk out on the pier. Cancelled 1914, $5-7.

After a 1919 fire destroyed Keating Pier and Casino, a new pier and casino was built. June 11, 1925 was the grand opening of the new $250,000 pier and casino. The pier was 1,208 feet long; and the ballroom in the ornate casino was 90 by 117 feet and accommodated 2,000 dancers. Through the years, top orchestras of the day—Wayne King, the Dorsey Brothers—were special attractions in addition to regular concerts in the casino. Circa 1930s, $3-5.

D-132   OCEAN PIER AND CASINO, DAYTONA BEACH, FLA.

4A-H2055

D.83.   VIEW OF PIER AND CASINO, DAYTONA BEACH, FLA.

110439

The Pier Casino. The sender of this postcard wrote, "Just took a ride of 30 miles on this beach and shook hands with J.D. Rockefeller." Cancelled 1927, $3-5.

LOOKING NORTH FROM OCEAN PIER, DAYTONA BEACH, FLORIDA—107

Parking your car at Daytona Beach's Boardwalk has always been popular, as shown in this view of the beach. In the year 2000, part of this beach became a "no car" zone. Circa 1920s, $5-7.

Cars on the beach just north of the
Clarendon Hotel, Circa 1920s, $5-7.

9847

Along the Beach, Daytona, Fla.

D-52. LOOKING SOUTH FROM OCEAN PIER,

SHOWING WIDTH OF MOST WONDERFUL BEACH IN THE WORLD. DAYTONA BEACH, FLA. 105363

Looking south on Daytona Beach from the Main Street Pier.
Cancelled 1928, $5-7.

Daytona Beach, Florida.
Fastest Automobile Race Course in the World.

On this beach in 1922, Sig Haughdahl drove his Wisconsin race car to a land speed record of 182.77 mph. Circa 1920s, $5-7.

Cars on the beach. Circa 1920s, $5-7.

Volusia County's first airport, the Daytona Beach Municipal Airport, opened May 15, 1930. On that day, a single-engine airplane took off, carrying the city's first night airmail to Jacksonville. That airport eventually evolved into Daytona Beach International Airport. Shown here is the airplane carrying the U.S. Mail. Cancelled 1933, $12-14.

THE WONDER BEACH OF THE WORLD, DAYTONA BEACH, FLORIDA—37

In 1931 "The World's Most Famous Beach" became the official slogan of Daytona Beach.
Automobile race drivers, tourists, residents and turtles all just love the beach. Circa 1930s, $5-7.

1A2225

Busy day at the beach, as the effects of the automobile revolution is plainly visible in this view of Daytona Beach. The car created new holiday resorts and the foundations of a vast tourist industry in Daytona Beach and many other Florida cities. Circa 1930s, $5-7.

HAVE A SWIM WITH US   S-315

PHOTO BY FRANK BELL   DAYTONA BEACH, FLA.   SA-H910

"BEAUTY AND THE BEACH"   S-320

DAYTONA BEACH, FLA.   SA-H1009

Beauty abounds on the beaches at Daytona Beach. Bathing suit fashions have changed since this view. A few years later two-piece bathing suits made their debut, and the beaches became much more crowded. Part of the success of Daytona Beach was due to eye-catching postcards such as this one. Cancelled 1940, $3-5.

This is the life! Playing in the surf at Daytona Beach, sunbathers find the golden sand and the warm water a welcome contrast as they vacation from the cold northern weather. Most of the year the water is suitable for water activities. Cancelled 1937, $2-4.

WACs on Parade, Daytona Beach, Fla.

PHOTO BY GRENELL

The Women's Army Corps (WAC) arrived in Daytona Beach in the fall of 1942. More than one hundred establishments were taken over to billet the women, and Tent City was established on Bethune Point. Daytona Beach suddenly became host to as many as 12,000 WACs at a time. This postcard shows WACs passing in review on the Daytona Beach Boardwalk. Circa 1943, $8-10.

Physical Training on the Beach
WAAC Training Center.
Daytona Beach, Fla.

Shown is the Women's Army Corps (WAC) training near the Boardwalk in 1943. An important part of basic training at the WAC Training Center was the physical exercises conducted on the beach. The 'fatigue' dresses were pale green and white striped seersucker. Hat and socks were khaki color that harmonized with the ocean and sand colors. Circa 1943, $2-4.

Ladies along the beach loved to show off their modern bathing suits. This view was taken on the beach side of the Sheraton Plaza Hotel (formerly the Clarendon Hotel). Circa 1940s, $1-3.

DB-52   BATHING SCENE AT DAYTONA THE WORLD'S MOST FAMOUS BEACH, SHERATON-PLAZA HOTEL IN BACKGROUND

Feeding sea gulls on the beach. Circa 1940s, $1-3.

A Red Cross Life Guard Station south of the Main Street Pier. Circa 1930s, $3-5.

Chapter Five
Racing on the Beach

In front of Clubhouse, Goodall, Fla., During Automobile races.

Since 1903, man and machine have been challenging speed in the Daytona Beach area. It began when the Winton Bullet won a Challenge Cup against the Olds Pirate on the Ormond Beach oceanfront. From 1927 to 1935 Henry Segrave and Sir Malcolm Campbell used area beaches to trade land speed records. Shown are spectators gathering on the beach in Goodall (became Daytona Beach in 1905). The Florida East Coast Automobile Clubhouse is shown on the left. Cancelled 1909, $22-24.

The 1903 racing meet on the beach racecourse was successful and led to the formation of the Florida East Coast Automobile Association whose purpose was to promote officially sanctioned beach races as an annual winter event. In 1904 the Association built a clubhouse at the Silver Beach approach in Goodall (now Daytona Beach) and this became the starting point for the races headed northward on the beach. Circa 1907, $15-17.

Crank 'er up and let's go for a spin! This group of motorists is going for a "joy ride" on the boulevard in front of the Florida East Coast Automobile Association Clubhouse. Circa 1908, $5-7.

Watching the Races, Daytona, Fla.

Spectators and contestants gather on the beach for the 1913 races. The sender of this card wrote, "Saw just such a crowd on Sunday, January 12, when Ruth Law went up in her airship. Wife and I each touched her airship." Circa 1913, $6-8.

On the Famous Ormond, Daytona Beach, Fla.

When automobile racing became the fad in the early 1900s, spectators rushed to the beach to watch the "gasoline guzzlers" roar and puff their way along the beach. The International speed trials were a great feature of the winter season and were held almost continuously until the mid 1930s. Circa 1910s. $6-8.

D.48 AUTO SPEED RACERS AT DAYTONA BEACH, FLA.

They're off! The flat white sand at Ormond and Daytona beaches were an internationally renowned racecourse at the turn of the twentieth century, a place for automobile manufacturers and race car drivers attempting to set new records for speed. Circa 1900s, $5-7.

The sender of this February 25 real photo postcard also took the picture shown of a racing car (in a cloud of dust) on the beach racecourse. Cancelled 1905, $20.

9141 THE "LINE UP."

DETROIT PUBLISHING CO.

Every car in Daytona Beach (all twenty-two of them) lined up for the publicity photograph on this postcard prior to the beach races in 1905. Circa 1907, $10-12.

Line up of Racing Cars at Daytona Beach, Fla.—61

Lineup of racing cars on the beach course, a 27-mile stretch of hard-packed sand on which the world's automobile records were broken year after year, in the early days of motoring, before anybody had ever thought of building a motor speedway. Circa, 1907, $8-10.

Famous Speed Racers on the Measured Mile, Daytona Beach, Fla.

THE MEASURED
MILE

FROM THIS POINT TO EXACTLY 5280
FEET TO THE SOUTH ALL THE FAMOUS
DAYTONA BEACH AUTOMOBILE INTER-
NATIONAL SPEED RECORDS HAVE BEEN SET.

THERE HAVE BEEN 80 OFFICIALLY
RECOGNIZED AUTOMOBILE SPEED RECORDS
ESTABLISHED ON THESE SANDS. HERE
WE CAN GIVE YOU BUT A FEW.

The Day	The Man	The Speed
March 7 1935	Sir Malcolm Campbell	276 M.P.H.
March 11 1929	Sir Henry Segrave	231 M.P.H.
April 27 1920	Tommy Milton	156 M.P.H.
Feb. 12 1919	Ralph de Palma	149 M.P.H.
March 16 1910	Barney Oldfield	131 M.P.H.
Jan. 27 1904	W. K. Vanderbilt	92 M.P.H.
Feb. 26 1903	Alexander Winton	68 M.P.H.

© CURT TEICH & CO., INC.

Stretching for twenty miles along the ocean, this silver beach known as nature's speedway is famous the world over as the home of high speed. Such famous men as Campbell, Segrave, Lockhart, De Palma and Oldfield have made speed history here. Shown in this postcard are the Bluebird V, Bluebird IV, Golden Arrow, Mystery-S, and Triplex. Circa 1930s, $20-22.

On March 29, 1927, English race driver Henry Segrave set the world speed record of 203.79 mph on the beach in a twin-aircraft engine 1,000-hp Sunbeam race car, the Mystery S. Upon Segrave's return to England, he was knighted as Sir Henry O'Neill DeHane Segrave. This was the first car in the world to break 200 mph. Circa 1920s, $20-22.

British driver Sir Malcolm Campbell set several world speed records on the beach. He upped the speed record to 206.96 in 1928 with his Napier aircraft-engine Bluebird. In 1931 Campbell set a 246.09 mph record, and a year later raised the record to 253.97 mph. Campbell owned sixteen different Bluebirds, each designed for maximum speed. Circa 1930s, $5-7.

D-139 BLUEBIRD DRIVEN TO A WORLD'S SPEED RECORD BY SIR MALCOLM CAMPBELL, DAYTONA BEACH, FLA.

PHOTO BY R. H. LE SESNE

5A-H439

On March 7, 1935, Sir Malcolm Campbell and his Bluebird V racing car made a record breaking run of 276.82 mph, which marked the limit of speed racing on the Ormond-Daytona Beach race course. Bluebird V's engine was the forerunner of the Merlin airplane engine to be used in the famous British World War II warplane, the Spitfire. Cancelled 1935, $23-25.

In 1933, Sir Malcolm Campbell drove his Bluebird IV racing car to a new world's speed record of 272.46 miles per hour. Cancelled 1935, $21-23.

A reproduction of a 1935 hand-colored postcard scene. This view shows the crew working on Sir Malcolm Campbell's Bluebird V near the old Clarendon Hotel prior to a run on the sands of Daytona Beach. His run in the flying mile still stands as the fastest record ever set on the beach. The Bluebird V is on display at Daytona International Speedway. Circa 1990, $1-3.

AEROPLANE VIEW OF RACE COURSE

It was 1947 when Bill France formed the National Association for Stock Car Auto Racing (NASCAR) and sanctioned racing began on the oval racing course just south of Daytona Beach in Ponce Inlet. It consisted of a back stretch that went north on the hard beach sands and then turned (North Turn) onto U. S. Highway A1A and headed south toward the South Turn, which headed back toward the beach. This was a crude but useful oval-shaped track. Stock car races were run on this combination sand-and-asphalt track for the next 20+ years. The narrow North Turn was the scene of many crashes. Circa 1930s, $1-3.

Daytona Beach and racing are almost synonymous. Since the early 1900s, Daytona Beach has hosted car races, which began on the beach and grew into the Daytona International Speedway; a postcard view is shown. Known as the "World Center of Racing," the speedway hosts NASCAR, sports car, motorcycle and go-kart races. The Daytona 500 is the most well known. The speedway, built in 1959, has grown into a very large motor sports complex. Circa 1959, $1-3.

The first motorcycle race was on a beach/road racecourse in 1937 and was called Daytona 200. The race kept getting bigger and more popular. Today the bike races are held at the Daytona International Speedway. Circa 1940s, $5-7.

This early 1960s helicopter view shows the start of the Daytona 500 race at the Daytona International Speedway. The track was considered to be the world's fastest closed track for automobile racing. Cancelled 1965, $8-10.

Chapter Six
Bridges and Ferry

This postcard, postmarked at Daytona on February 20, shows a view looking west over North Bridge and Halifax River toward mainland Daytona. This is how the western end of Ocean Boulevard (became Seabreeze Boulevard in 1939) looked at the time. Cancelled 1915, $2-4.

Ocean Boulevard, Seabreeze, Daytona, Fla.

FERRY TO DAYTONA BEACH

In 1903, Captain Leon E. Ellenwood started a ferryboat business that ran from Volusia Avenue (now International Speedway Boulevard) and Beach Street to a peninsula landing at the foot of Main Street. The ferry ride cost 10¢. The names of the ferryboats were Yankee Doodle and Dixie. This was also the landing for the excursion steamer Cherokee, which took visitors on cruises up the Halifax and Tomoka rivers. Cancelled 1909, $8-10.

Seabreeze, Fla., North Bridge & The Halifax River.

Looking west over North Bridge and the Halifax River from the western end of Ocean Boulevard (now Seabreeze Boulevard) in the town of Seabreeze. This wooden bridge, built in 1902, joined Seabreeze with mainland Daytona.
Cancelled 1909, $10-12.

Shown is the home of C. C. and Helen Wilmans Post on the Halifax River at the foot of Ocean Boulevard (now Seabreeze Boulevard). The Posts bought one-half interest in the property of Charles A. Ballough and platted the Town of Seabreeze (now part of Daytona Beach), which Mrs. Post named "The City Beautiful." Said to be one of the finest homes in the state south of St. Augustine, it later became the Bellevue-Halifax Hotel. It was demolished in 1959. The Diplomat Center now occupies the site.
Circa 1905, $2-4.

MIDDLE BRIDGE AND THE HOME OF MRS. POST, SEA BREEZE, FLA.

E. C. KROPP, PUBL., MILWAUKEE, NO. 3069

Middle Bridge, Between Daytona & Daytona Beach, Fla.

1909

Approach to one of the early bridges leading from the mainland, across the Halifax River, to the
Atlantic Ocean and beaches. Cancelled 1909, $10-12.

New Concrete Bridge across the Halifax River at Daytona, Fla.

The "Concrete Bridge" looking east from Beach Street. Note the streetcar tracks on the right side of the bridge. This bridge was later known as the Broadway Bridge. Circa 1930s, $10-12.

Streetcar crossing the Concrete Bridge. Circa 1930s, $6-8.

New Concrete Bridge across the Halifax River, at Daytona, Fla.

South Bridge, constructed of wood planking in 1888 by the St. Johns and Halifax River Railroad Company, connected Orange and Silver Beach avenues. The first building on the left is the Railroad Depot, at the corner of Orange Avenue and Beach Street, built in 1887. Henry Flagler, who helped finance the bridge, ran a spur line to the bridge to make connection with the steamboats plying the Halifax River. The third building on the left is Daytona's first public library. Circa 1909, $10-12.

Daytona, Florida. Entrance to South Bridge, showing City Hall.

The Water Front, Daytona, Fla.

206, 493. J.V.

Daytona's waterfront in 1910. The steamboat Swan made trips to Palm Beach from the South Bridge dock (where the City Fire Department building is now). The Swan was a three-deck, 156-foot stern-wheeler that could carry up to eighty passengers and forty cars. Shown in this view is South Bridge, the Daytona City Hall building (left of the bridge) and Daytona's first public library (on the right). Cancelled 1913, $5-7.

D.81. AERIAL VIEW OF BEACH STREET AND WATER FRONT PARK, DAYTONA BEACH, FLA.

110437

This postcard shows the four main bridges in Daytona Beach. South Bridge and City Island are shown in the bottom bridge.
Circa 1930s, $1-3.

This wooden bridge, constructed in 1906, crossed Halifax River at Port Orange, a village established in 1866 and named because of the citrus culture. Cancelled 1908, $6-8.

Port Orange, Fla.   New Port Orange Bridge.

85

Chapter Seven
Business and Industry

Business Center of Beach Street, Daytona, Fla.

Most of Daytona's early businesses were located on the west side of Beach Street. Here residents and tourists could find banks, post office, hardware stores, hotels, department stores and a variety of other businesses. Circa 1910s, $4-6.

In 1896, the Merchants Bank was built on the corner of Beach and Magnolia streets. In 1910, the bank occupied the building on Beach Street that currently houses the Halifax Historical Museum. This 1911 postcard produced for the bank illustrates the popularity of the postcard as a convenient means of advertising. Cancelled 1911, $5-7.

New City Hall, Daytona, Fla.—58

Daytona's third City Hall was built at the corner of Orange and Palmetto avenues. This structure was first occupied in 1921, with the Daytona Public Library located on the second floor of the building. Circa 1920s, $3-5.

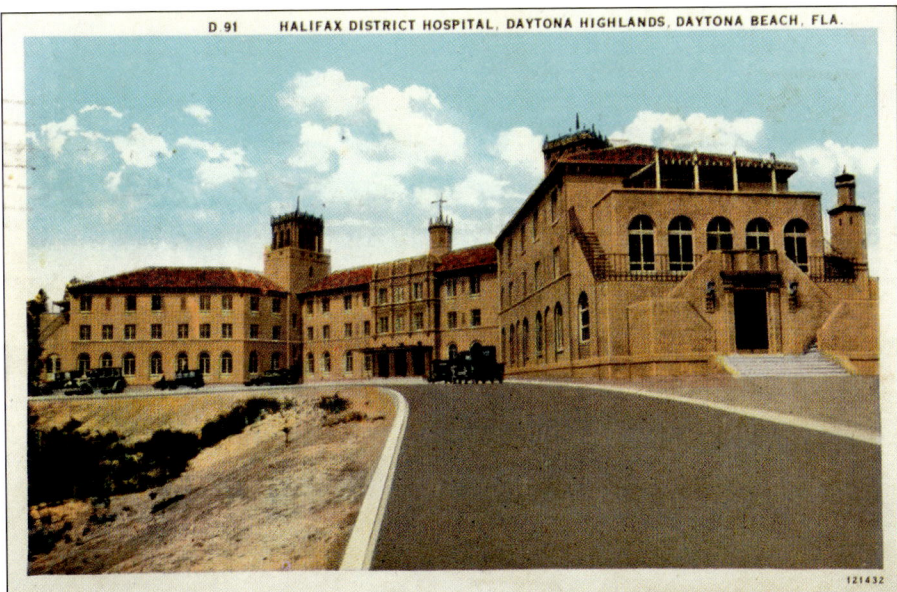

D 91   HALIFAX DISTRICT HOSPITAL, DAYTONA HIGHLANDS, DAYTONA BEACH, FLA.

A view of the 125-bed Halifax Hospital when it opened in 1928. Cancelled 1932, $3-5.

DB-95   HALIFAX HOSPITAL, DAYTONA BEACH, FLORIDA

The Halifax Hospital, located at the intersection of Clyde Morris and International Speedway boulevards, is the largest hospital in the area. Today, it is a much larger complex than shown here. Circa 1930s, $2-4.

Halifax District Hospital, Daytona Beach, Florida

During World War II, the Halifax Hospital was the first building to be occupied by the Women's Army Corps (WAC). During 1944-1946 it was known as the U.S. Army Welch Convalescent Center. Circa 1930s, $1-3.

UNITED STATES POST OFFICE, DAYTONA BEACH, FLORIDA—69

The U.S. Post Office on Beach Street, designed by local architect Harry M. Griffin in 1932, is in the Spanish Renaissance style. Built of bog stone from the Florida Keys, with a red terra-cotta tile roof, its most eye-catching feature is the seven gargoyles peering out from below the roofline. The building interior has a lobby of Tennessee marble and interesting wrought iron grills. Circa 1930s, $4-6.

The S.H. Kress building, shown on the right side of the postcard, is a 75-year old Art Deco structure at 140 S. Beach Street. Designed by architect Edward F. Sibbert, the building uses the same design feature found in many other old Kress stores. Originally a Five-and-Dime store, the landmark structure is now used as an office building. It was added to the National Register of Historic Places in 1983. Circa 1932, $1-3.

D-120   BEACH STREET, LOOKING SOUTH, DAYTONA BEACH, FLA.

PHOTO BY R. H. LE SESNE

U. S. Post Office and Waterfront Park,
Daytona Beach, Florida   2

On August 11, 1933, the United States Post Office building on Beach Street was dedicated and for almost seven decades has been an object of admiration for Daytona Beach visitors from throughout America. This view was taken from Riverfront Park. Circa 1930s, $2-4.

D.67. F.E.C. RAILROAD STATION, DAYTONA BEACH, FLORIDA.

105583

In 1924, Daytona's second railway station, of Spanish Renaissance style architecture, was built on Magnolia Avenue. The station was constructed of brick, finished with stucco and a trim of red brick, with a tile roof. Several of the waiting rooms had marble floors. The train station was demolished in 1984. Circa 1920s, $10-12.

The Depot, Daytona, Fla.

Henry M. Flagler bought the St. Johns and Halifax River Railroad, changed the name to Florida East Coast Railway, extended the railroad south, and built Daytona's second train depot. Platforms extended from the freight depot on Volusia Avenue (now International Speedway Boulevard) to the passenger depot at Magnolia Avenue. This new train depot replaced the old Orange Avenue passenger depot, which became Daytona's second City Hall. Circa 1920s, $12-14.

F. E. C. Depot, Daytona, Fla.

A view of a FEC passenger train stopped at the Daytona terminal. Circa 1924, $10-12.

This postcard of a Florida East Coast Railway Streamliner is a reminder of the glamorous, exciting age of railway travel when these "Iron horses" roared over the tracks, bringing many thousands of visitors and settlers to Daytona Beach and other parts of Florida. Circa 1930s, $4-6.

Streamliner on the Florida East Coast Daytona Beach, Fla.

DB-97 FLORIDA EAST COAST STREAMLINER ARRIVING AT DAYTONA BEACH, FLORIDA

A Florida East Coast Railway Streamliner arriving at the Daytona Beach station on Magnolia Avenue. This station was one of the finest stations south of Jacksonville in appearance, finish, furnishings, and in facilities. The railway company offered passenger service until 1963 before switching entirely to carrying freight. Circa 1940s, $8-10.

YOWELL-DREW-IVEY CO.

Daytona Beach, Fla.

The Yowell-Drew-Ivey Company
Department Store at the corner of
Beach Street and Magnolia Avenue.
It later became Dunn's Toy Store.
Cancelled 1944, $1-3.

The Papaya Farm at Daytona Beach, a mile south of
Silver Beach Avenue on the peninsula, was a novelty
for tourists. This tropical fruit eaten for breakfast,
dessert, and in salads was also used to make jams,
ice creams, crystallized fruit and canned in syrup.
The fruit also had medicinal properties used to
cure stomach disorders. Circa 1930s, $1-3.

812   A PAPAYA PLANTATION IN FLORIDA

DAYTONA BEACH, FLA.

3A-H685

Chapter Eight

Parks and Gardens

Daytona, Florida, Hoehne Park, Private Grounds, Along Ridgewood Avenue

Hoehne Park, a private exotic park along Ridgewood Avenue, was located at the home of the Hoehne family, Circa 1910s, $1-3.

A bird's eye view of City Island Ball Park. Built in 1914, it was the site of the first racially integrated Spring Training game in baseball history, occurring on March 17, 1946. The historic game featured the Brooklyn Dodgers and Jackie Robinson and the Montreal Royals, the Brooklyn Dodgers farm team. Robinson was not allowed to play in Sanford and St. Augustine. In 1990, the ballpark was renovated and named the Jackie Robinson Ball Park. Circa 1940s, $3-5.

City Island, Recreation Center, Daytona Beach, Fla.

City Island Dock and Recreation Center, Daytona Beach, Fla.

Looking east over the Orange Avenue Bridge at the City Island Dock and Recreation Center, the City Island Ball Park is shown on the north side of Orange Avenue. Circa 1930s, $1-3.

FOOT BRIDGE, IN WATERFRONT PARK, DAYTONA BEACH, FLORIDA — 5

In the mid 1920s, the area east of the Esplanada on Beach Street, extending from Orange Avenue to Fairview Avenue was filled in and Riverfront Park was created. Henry Stockman, a well-known landscape architect, came to Daytona to develop the park. Circa 1930s, $1-3.

This view shows Beach Street businesses on the left and the beautifully landscaped Riverfront Park on the right. This is one of the most picturesque parks in the area and, throughout the years, has been used for a variety of social events. Circa 1930s, $1-3.

Riverfront Park lies on one side of Beach Street; shops and stores are on the other side of the street. Beach Street has always been the heart of Daytona's shopping district. Circa 1930s, $1-3.

Gorgeous goldfish play amidst subtropical water lilies and bubbling fountains of the many pools in the mile long Riverfront Park in downtown Daytona Beach. Circa 1930s, $1-3.

Beach Street from Beautiful Waterfront Park, Daytona Beach, Fla.

Shoppers in the stores on Beach Street always enjoyed the beautiful vista in Riverfront Park. Circa 1930s, $1-3.

Scenic Waterfront Park, Showing American Legion Memorial Fountain, Daytona Beach, Fla.

The American Legion Memorial Fountain was first located in Daytona Beach's Riverfront Park on Beach Street. It was built in 1932 and donated to the city by Mrs. Lillian B. Dana. The tablet in front reads: "To the American Legion in memory of their deceased comrades and those who remain to serve." The fountain was moved to the Orange Avenue entrance to Tuscawilla Park. Circa 1930s, $1-3.

Chapter Nine
Along the Halifax River

The Halifax River is part of the Intercoastal Waterway, a 1,200-mile-long sheltered route extending from Boston to Key West. It consists of rivers, inland bays, canals, inlets, and estuaries. This view of Halifax River is south from the Halifax River Yacht Club. Circa 1910s, $4-6.

Halifax River S. from Yacht Club, Daytona, Fla.

Daytona. Fla. Yacht Club.

The Halifax River Yacht Club, built in 1896, is located on Halifax River just south of the intersection of Beach Street and Orange Avenue. In 2005 the historic clubhouse was replaced with a larger, Key West style clubhouse. Circa 1905, $8-10.

Halifax River N. Beach St. a Bay St., DAYTONA Fla.

3203.

This postcard shows Halifax River as seen from the corner of North Beach and Bay streets. Circa 1904, $1-3.

Daytona, Florida. Glimpse of the Water Front.

A glimpse of the Halifax River showing Gilles Dock in the center. In the late 1800s and early 1900s, several excursion boats and launches took tourists up the Halifax and Tomoka rivers. The names of some of the boats were Belle Harbor, Cherokee, Nemo, Princess Issena, Southland, Sun Tan, Tomoka, Uncle Sam, Halifax, Columbia and Nina Poncheo. These boats made daily trips, often stopping for lunch at a remote cabin on the Upper Tomoka River. Many of the boat trips started at Gilles Dock. Circa 1900s, $3-5.

8144. WATER FRONT, DAYTONA, FLA.   COPYRIGHT, 1904, BY DETROIT PHOTOGRAPHIC CO.

Passengers are boarding an excursion boat for a trip on the Halifax River. Shown in the center background is Daytona's first train depot. Copyright 1904, $5-7.

Pleasure Boat, "Uncle Sam", on her celebrated Palm Beach Trip, Daytona, Fla.

The Uncle Sam was operated by the McCoy Brothers and made three Tomoka River trips weekly from Gilles Dock. Round trip cost was $1. The Uncle Sam also made round-trip excursion trips to Palm Beach. Cancelled 1908, $6-8.

Daytona, Florida. Excursion Boat "Constitution" at the Dock.

The excursion boat Constitution at the dock at Daytona. This steamer runs southward to Palm Beach on inland waterways (now the Intercoastal Waterway). Cancelled 1911, $10-12.

Royal Poinciana, Palm Beach, Fla.

Rockledge, Fla.   New Rockledge Hotel.

Nothing in the whole history of the Intercoastal Waterway was ever so picturesque and romantic as the steamboats. These boats operated between Jacksonville and Palm Beach. The names of some of the steamboats were Santa Lucia, Sweeney, St. Augustine, Georgiana, Swan, Dutchess, Greenwich, Indian River, Nellie Hudson, Progress, and City of Monticello. Circa 1910s, $3-5.

During the late 1800s and early 1900s, popular steamboat stopping points between Jacksonville and Palm Beach were St. Augustine, Daytona and Rockledge. This postcard shows the Rockledge Hotel, one of the fashionable winter resorts along the Intercoastal Waterway. Circa 1908, $12-14.

Port Orange, Fla.   Looking down the Halifax.

This postcard shows the west end of the wooden Port Orange Bridge that was built in 1906. The one-mile toll bridge crossed the Halifax River. Cancelled 1910, $8-10.

Dr. John M. Hawks bought property here in 1865 and settled it about 1872, naming it Hawks Park. The name was changed to Edgewater in 1924. It is located south of Daytona Beach. This postcard of the Bayview House is located along the Indian River, a continuation of the Intercoastal Waterway south of the Halifax River. Cancelled 1908, $12-14.

Bayview House, Hawks Park, near New Smyrna, Fla.

A typical moonlight view of the Halifax River at Daytona. Cancelled 1913, $2-4.

MOONLIGHT ON THE HALIFAX RIVER, DAYTONA, FLA.

VIEW ACROSS THE HALIFAX RIVER TOWARDS SEABREEZE, DAYTONA, FLA.

A postcard view across the Halifax River toward Seabreeze (now part of Daytona Beach). The Halifax River is an arm of the sea, separated from the Atlantic Ocean by a narrow strip of land called the Halifax Peninsula. The river and its connecting creeks and lagoons have always provided ideal boating for residents and visitors alike. Circa 1910, $3-5.

AEROPLANE VIEW OF BEACH STREET, DAYTONA BEACH, FLORIDA

Beach Street has always been regarded as one of the world's most beautiful business thoroughfares. This bird's-eye view of the southern sector shows the Halifax River Yacht Club area with several boats on the river. Waterfowl often gathered here to be fed daily by residents and visitors. Circa 1920s, $3-5.

A RESTFUL SPOT ON THE HALIFAX RIVER, DAYTONA, FLA.

A restful spot along the Halifax River. Cancelled 1914, $3-5.

Yacht Basin and Boat Works, Daytona Beach, Fla.

Daytona Marina and Boat Works located on South Beach Street and the Halifax River. A special dredged channel brings boats in from the Intercoastal Waterway (Halifax River). This business has had a colorful history that started in 1903, and in the 1920s and 1930s, it was not uncommon to have many yachts of 100 feet or more in berth at the same time. During World War II, nineteen sub-chasing boats were built here along with several air-sea rescue vessels and motor launches. To this day, the facility continues to be a favorite haven for boaters traveling the Intercoastal Waterway. Circa 1930s, $1-3.

DB-3   SAILBOATS ON HALIFAX RIVER, DAYTONA BEACH, FLORIDA

The Halifax River is often dotted with the sails of many craft. Shown is a scene of the annual Florida State sailboat regatta, sponsored by the Daytona Beach Sailboat Club. Boating on the Halifax has always been a popular activity, from steamboats in the 1800s to today's jet-watercraft. Circa 1930s, $1-3.

Turtle Mound at Sunrise on the Indian River near New Smyrna Beach, Fla.

In prehistoric times the Timucua Indians inhabited the entire northeast Florida area and were builders of large shell mounds. The fifty-foot high Turtle Mound (shown here), south of Daytona Beach, was known as far back as 1564 and for years it was marked on ship's maps as an aid to navigation. It is the largest Indian mound in the state. Circa 1930, $1-3.

Chapter Ten
Schools and Churches

Daytona Public School, Daytona, Fla.

A view of the Bay Street School, located at Bay Street and Palmetto Avenue. This school, erected in 1909, was later renamed as Daytona High School, then Mainland Senior High School and finally Mainland Junior High School. Mainland Junior High School closed in 1983 and the building was eventually torn down. Cancelled 1912, $10-12.

The sender of this card of the Bay Street School marked an X on the postcard to indicate the first grade classroom. The other first grade classroom was across the hall on the first floor. Cancelled 1910, $10-12.

PUBLIC SCHOOL, DAYTONA, FLA.

Seabreeze High School, on the corner of Grandview Avenue and Earl Street, opened for the 1917-18 school year. In 1962 a new Seabreeze High School was built. The building shown in this Real Photo Postcard became Seabreeze Junior High, which closed in 1983; later the building was demolished. Circa 1920s, $10-12.

SEABREEZE HIGH SCHOOL ~ DAYTONA BEACH, FLA. 3742

One of the most beautiful buildings in the area was known as the interfaith Tourist Church for years. Designed by Harry M. Griffin in California Mission style in 1930, it is built of 'bog rock' that was mined near an area where prehistoric fossils have been discovered. The church changes color as the sun plays off the rock at different times of the day. It is now called the Seabreeze United Church. Cancelled 1939, $1-3.

The Tourist Church, Daytona Beach, Florida

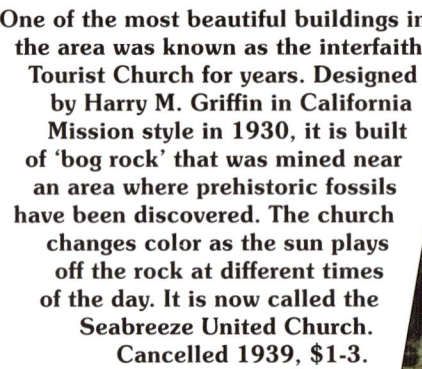

BETHUNE-COOKMAN COLLEGE — Daytona Beach, Florida

Bethune-Cookman College is a four-year, church-related (Methodist) coeducational college, created as the result of a merger in 1924 of the Cookman Institute for Boys of Jacksonville and the Daytona Normal and Industrial School for Girls, founded by internationally acclaimed educator Mary McLeod Bethune. The college campus occupies 60 acres near the heart of Daytona Beach and includes many well-equipped, attractive buildings. Shown in this postcard is Faith Hall. Circa 1930s, $12-14.

Saint Mary's Episcopal Church, at the corner of Orange and Ridgewood avenues, was the first church built in Daytona (1883). The structure has been remodeled and added to many times since it was built, but always in keeping with the original architecture. Cancelled 1912, $3-5.

In 1892, the First Methodist Church, on the corner of Bay Street and Palmetto Avenue, opened for service. In 1904, the church became interested in Mary McLeod Bethune's school and appropriated substantial money for its support. The church shown in this 1916 postcard was demolished in 1927. In 1952 a new sanctuary was built in the same location. Cancelled 1916, $4-6.

The First Congregational Church was located amid palmetto and other evergreens at the corner of Volusia (now International Speedway Boulevard) and Palmetto avenues. In 1885, the first services were held in this facility. Circa 1910s, $3-5.

107

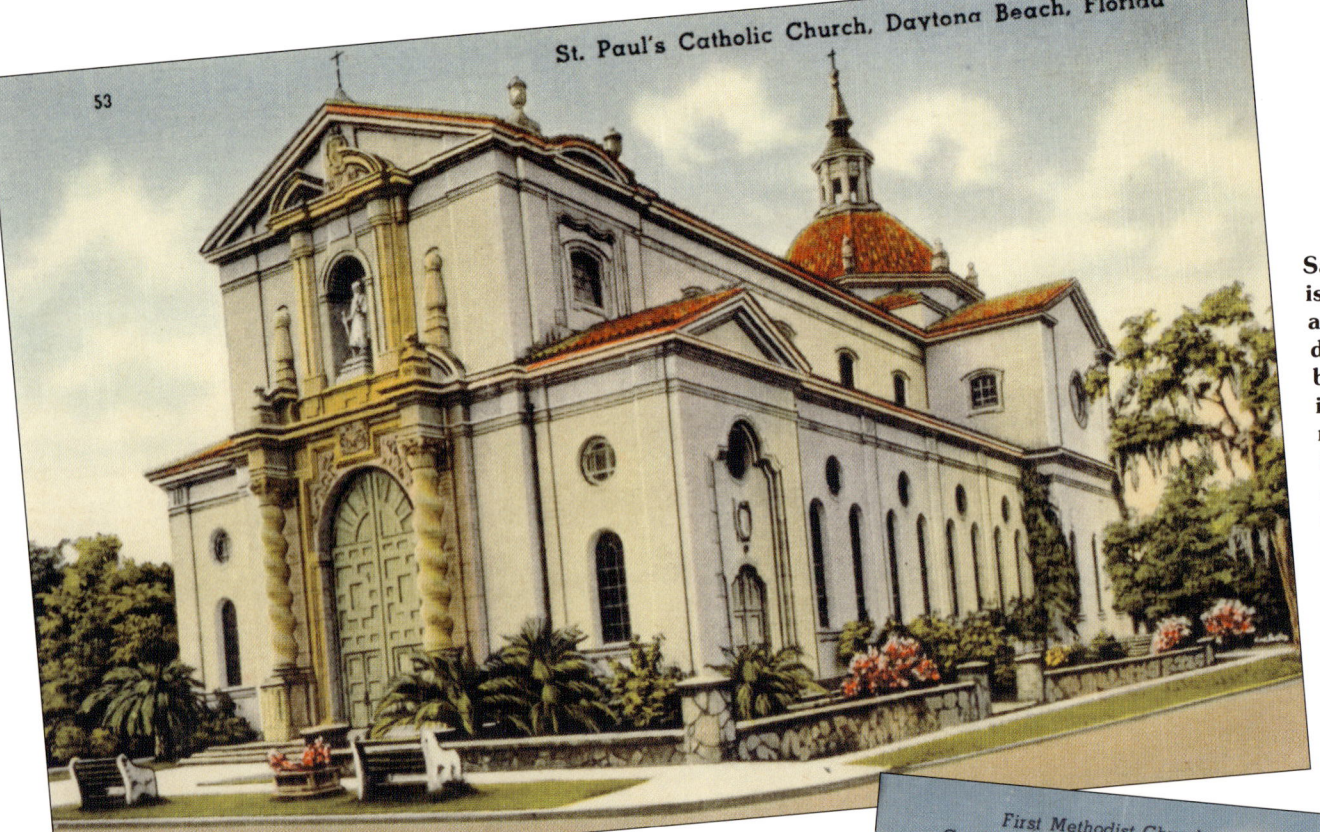

St. Paul's Catholic Church, Daytona Beach, Florida

Saint Paul's Catholic Church, built in 1927, is very impressive with its stucco exterior, art stone trim, beautiful tiled roof and dome, and gilded cross. It was the highest building on the mainland at the time of its completion. The pillared entrance with massive doors, replicas of the basilica in Valencia, Spain, fronts on Ridgewood Avenue. The interior, with a seating capacity for 1,000 people, although smaller, is an exact replica of the Saint Patrick's Cathedral in New York City. Circa 1930s, $3-5.

First Methodist Church was organized in 1877. The first church building was completed in 1892; the present sanctuary was completed in 1952. This structure is one of the outstanding church buildings in Florida. The congregation voted to close the church in early 2001. Circa 1950s, $1-3.

First Methodist Church
Corner of Palmetto and Bay Streets
Daytona Beach, Florida

The Church with the Singing Tower
First Baptist Church of
Daytona Beach, Florida

107

First Baptist Church of
Daytona Beach, the church
with the Singing Tower.
Circa 1930s, $1-3.

DB-17 COMMUNITY METHODIST EPISCOPAL CHURCH, DAYTONA BEACH, FLORIDA

Community Methodist Episcopal Church. Circa 1930s, $1-3.

Port Orange Fla. The Episcopal
Church and Ridgewood Hall

The Grace Episcopal Church, located at 4100 Ridgewood Avenue in Port
Orange, was built in 1893 in the Gothic Revival architectural style. Design
features of this church include a pitched roof and a bell tower, with a flared
hip roof and belfry skirt along the facade. Today this church is a beautiful
example of historic preservation. Circa 1909, $14-16.

Chapter Eleven
Recreation

This postcard scene shows a daily catch of fish in the Daytona Beach area. Circa 1904, $3-5.

Boating around the Halifax River Yacht Club was a popular activity. Cancelled 1913, $5-7.

A morning catch of sharks at Seabreeze (now Daytona Beach).
Cancelled 1907, $10-12.

A Mornings Catch at Seabreeze, Fla.

111

FISHING FROM THE PIER. DAYTONA BEACH, FLORIDA.

Pier fishing has always been
a popular activity in the
Daytona Beach area.
Circa 1907, $3-5.

New $40,000 Auditorium, Daytona Beach and Seabreeze, Fla.—69

D-47 FISHING IN THE ATLANTIC OCEAN, END OF PIER, DAYTONA BEACH, FLA.

103491

The original wooden Peabody Auditorium, built in 1919 on land donated
by Simon J. Peabody, established itself as a cultural focus for residents of
Daytona Beach. This auditorium was destroyed by fire on January 7, 1946; in
1949, a new auditorium was built at the same location. Cancelled 1926, $4-6.

Fishing on the Main Street Pier. Cancelled 1933, $1-3.

D-55. PEPPS POOL, DAYTONA BEACH, FLA., CASINO BUILDING IN REAR.

105365

Pepp's Pool, the finest and largest swimming pool on the East Coast of Florida, was located just south of the Main Street Pier. It was the first swimming pool in the area. Six-year-old Florence, daughter of Harry Pepper, owner of the pool, was the first person to dive off the second tower of the pool. Angie Green, daughter of the pool architect and contractor, together with D. F. Fuquay, dove off the top tower. The pool closed in 1937. Circa 1925, $5-7.

Looking southwest from the roof of the Main Street Pier Casino. Pepp's Pool shown in the foreground, the Breakers Hotel and Daytona Beach Hotel are shown in the background. Circa 1925, $5-7.

D-56. VIEW FROM ATLANTIC OCEAN, DAYTONA BEACH, FLA.

SHOWING REAR VIEW PEPPS POOL AND BEACH REST BUILDINGS.

105360

2753-30

Since 1904, shuffleboard has been a popular activity for people visiting Florida. The first game in America was played on the sidewalk of the Lyndhurst Hotel in Daytona. Circa 1920s, $3-5.

In the 1930s and 1940s illegal casinos operated in Daytona Beach, undisturbed by the city or the police. Some of the most popular gambling spots were the Chateau Lido, Trocadero Club, Charlie's Hi Hat Club, and Seabreeze Golf and Tennis Club. Elegant restaurants, slot machines, roulette wheels with tuxedoed croupiers, crap tables, and blackjack tables offered "Las Vegas excitement" for Daytona Beach visitors long before Las Vegas became popular. This postcard portrays the Hi-Hat Club, which was on the second story of Charlie's Grill & Cocktail Bar, located at 308 Seabreeze Boulevard. Circa 1930s, $18-20.

Charlie's GRILL & COCKTAIL BAR

BPOE

FISHING

GOLF

HI-HAT CLUB

RACING ON THE BEACH

D.122 THRONGS ENJOYING THE OCEAN PROMENADE, DAYTONA BEACH, FLA.

PHOTO BY R. H. LE SESNE

3A-H879

Crowds stroll and enjoy the sunshine on Daytona Beach's ocean promenade, the Boardwalk. The Clarendon Hotel is shown in the far distance. Cancelled 1934, $1-3.

These centuries-old saurians (alligators and crocodiles to most people) are shown basking in the warm sunshine in a native jungle beauty spot at Tropical Park in South Daytona. Some of these "gators" did tricks for the entertainment of winter and summer visitors. The park, on Ridgewood Avenue (U.S. 1) at the intersection of Big Tree Road, was also, at one time, called the Daytona Beach Alligator Farm and included the original collection of "Alligator Joe" Campbell. Cancelled 1938, $4-6.

K131—ALLIGATOR FARM, TROPICAL PARK, DAYTONA BEACH, FLORIDA

R. H. LESESNE PHOTO

Memorial Stadium, Daytona Beach, Florida

100

Y. M. C. A., DAYTONA BEACH, FLORIDA—K49

Daytona Beach's first Y.M.C.A. was located on Beach Street. It had many facilities for fun and health, Circa 1940s, $3-5.

The Memorial Stadium, located near the Daytona Beach Community College campus, was the center of most sporting activities in Daytona Beach until the 1990s. Circa 1940s, $1-3.

Snapper fishing with Captain Frank Timmons aboard the "Marianne" was a popular activity in Daytona Beach. Shown in the background is the Ponce de Leon Inlet Lighthouse. Circa 1940s, $3-5.

El Patio Marino, located on Daytona Beach's Boardwalk, is where thousands enjoyed wining, dining, and dancing under the stars, to the music of fine orchestras. Cancelled 1939, $3-5.

Thousands of fans gathered at the Volusia County Kennel Club (now the Daytona Beach Kennel Club) nightly. Circa 1940s, $1-3.

The Snack Bar at the Youth Council Patio on Daytona Beach's Boardwalk. This facility was open every day and evening exclusively for teenagers who wanted to dance, lounge, play pool, play ping-pong, play shuffleboard, and swim. Circa 1940s, $3-5.

They call Jai-Alai the fastest game on two feet, and it is one of the oldest ball games in the world. The game is played in a large arena called a fronton. Jai Alai (pronounced hi-li) originated in the Pyrenees Mountains of northern Spain during the 15th century. Daytona Beach opened its fronton in 1959. Six months a year, thousands of excited spectators viewed Jai Alai players in action. Circa 1959, $3-5.

The Daytona Beach Jai-Alai fronton was considered by the sports experts to have the finest and fastest court in the world. Specially fabricated 12-inch thick blocks of Georgia granite were installed to assure perfection. The fast rock-hard ball traveled at better than 170 miles per hour. Circa 1959, $3-5.

Sea Zoo, located two miles south of Daytona Beach in South Daytona, was originally the Marine Life Laboratory founded in 1949 by M.S. Bangs and Stephen Loughman. In 1951, with the addition of Dr. Perry Sperber, a partnership was formed creating Sea Zoo. The nine-acre roadside attraction on Ridgewood Avenue (U.S. Highway 1) became a popular stop for tourists. It expanded during the 1950s to include alligator wrestling, a snake pit, porpoise show and tropical bird display. Circa 1950s, $6-8.

Jim Rusing Ski Show in Lake Lloyd at the Daytona International Speedway featured boat jumping through a wall of fire, world's only water skiing carousel horse (shown here), and many other action-packed acts. Circa 1960s, $5-7.

Chapter Twelve
Coquina Structures

The Tarragonna Tower in this postcard shows the medieval entrance to Coquina Highlands, a housing development later renamed Daytona Highlands. The tower, built of coquina rock quarried on the property, contained a lecture room, a storage room, a drafting room, and a lookout. Later, many of the lovely lakes were filled and the hills flattened to make way for the present Mainland High School. Today, the Tower on International Speedway Boulevard has been reduced to only one arch, however, many of the lovely Spanish style homes built in the mid-1920s still remain. Cancelled 1928, $1-3.

D.66. TARRAGONA TOWER, MEDIEVAL ENTRANCE TO DAYTONA HIGHLANDS, DAYTONA BEACH, FLORIDA.

"FLORIDA'S SUBURB OF HILLS AND LAKES".

105582

Spanish Arch entrance to the Ocean Promenade at Daytona Beach, the coquina pedestrian bridge shown allowed people to walk from the boardwalk to the Main Street Pier and Casino. Circa 1930s, $3-5.

Summer or winter, there is always something to do on the World's Most Famous Beach. Shown is the Women's Army Corps (WAC) exercising on the beach at the Boardwalk. The WAC training center was officially discontinued in Daytona Beach in March 1944. In the background you can see the Clock Tower (on the left), the Bandshell (on the right), and the Clarendon Hotel (on the far right). Circa 1942, $1-3.

Bathing in Atlantic Ocean surf has always been popular with Daytona Beach visitors. In the area of the Boardwalk the bathers were under the watchful eye of the Red Cross Lifeguards who worked out of this coquina rock station behind the Band shell. A staff of 35 lifeguards manned eighteen stations along the beach. Circa 1950s, $4-6.

Coquina is a stone-like substance formed by nature from shells, mostly of coquina and oyster shell fragments. Because of its rich lime content it can be converted to a mortar-like substance called 'tabby'. Deposits of coquina appear as occasional rocks, groups of rocks, or in a mass large enough to be quarried. Coquina and oyster shells were early road building materials. Through the years, coquina has been widely used in the Daytona Beach area. Many local homes, city buildings, fences and structures are constructed of coquina. Shown here is the Bandshell that was built of coquina rock and opened with much fanfare on July 4, 1937. Circa 1930s, $1-3.

World's Largest Bandshell and Open-Air Theater, Daytona Beach, Fla.

Daytona Beach's Open Air Bandshell, built as part of a Works Progress Administration (WPA) project, has hosted hundreds of band concerts, social events, dances, and other entertainment events. It is one of the world's largest open-air theaters. Circa 1930s, $1-3.

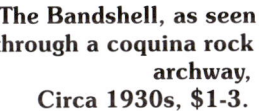

Band Shell Seen Through the Arch of the Fountain Daytona Beach, Fla.

The Bandshell, as seen through a coquina rock archway, Circa 1930s, $1-3.

CLOCK TOWER, DAYTONA BEACH, FLORIDA

The Clock Tower, built of coquina rock on Daytona Beach's Boardwalk in 1936, has a unique clock face in that it uses the letters DAYTONA BEACH instead of numerals. The beautiful tower still graces the Boardwalk along with its neighboring structure, the Bandshell. If it is 25 minutes past 9 o'clock, it is 'C' after 'D' by the quaint coquina Clock Tower at the beach. Circa 1930s, $1-3.

Chapter Thirteen
Potpourri

The Big Tree was once the Indians' council tree beneath whose spreading limbs the tribes gathered to make medicine. In 1877, when the town of Blake (now South Daytona) was first settled, its main street was Big Tree Road—named because in the midst of the Leach Brother's orange grove grew a giant oak tree with a circumference of 35 feet, and a height of over 100 feet. Its branches, with a spread of 157 feet were so huge and strong that steps were built up to a pavilion (or tree house). The tree eventually became a tourist attraction. Today, nothing remains of the Big Tree. Circa 1906, $5-7.

Daytona, Fla. A Three branch Palmetto Tree.

Daytona, Fla., big tree, circumference 35 feet.

On the northwest corner of Volusia (now International Speedway Boulevard) and Ridgewood avenues, there once grew a Three-branched Palm Tree that was quite a curiosity to tourists. It was pictured from every angle on postcards of the early 1900s. As Volusia and Ridgewood avenues were widened, the tree was moved to the City Hall where it eventually died. The unusual tree was once listed by Ripley's "Believe It Or Not" as the only one of its kind in the world. Today, a smaller three-branched Palm Tree may be seen in the Sugar Mill Botanical Gardens in Port Orange. Circa 1907, $6-8.

Port Orange, Fla. Ruin Old Spanish Sugar Mill. Built 1705.

The Nineteenth Century Sugar Mill Ruins at Sugar Mill Botanical Gardens in Port Orange are probably the most complete and best preserved ruins of their kind in America. The old English Sugar Mill ruins have machinery still intact because the mill operated up through the Civil War and almost to the 1900s. The Sugar Mill ruins are on the National Register of Historic Places. Circa 1908, $6-8.

The Beauty of Daytona Beach,
"The Lighthouse"

The Ponce de Leon Inlet Lighthouse, south of Daytona Beach, was the first lighthouse in Florida to be designated a National Historic Landmark. Standing 175 feet high, the 1887 lighthouse is the nation's tallest lighthouse, among those that remain on their original sites. The original lighthouse used a kerosene lamp to light the fixed Frensel lens. Its light could be spotted from twenty miles out to sea. Circa 1930s, $1-3.

S.617 Old Spanish Sugar House - Built 1705,
Fort Orange near Daytona, Florida.

Patrick Dean, who was granted 995 acres by the Spanish government in 1804, established the first sugar mill at Port Orange. The plantation changed hands twice before it was burned down in 1836 during the Second Seminole War. It was rebuilt in 1846 by John Marchall, who converted the refining process to steam. The Sugar Mill ruins are illustrated on this Alligator Border postcard. Cancelled 1908, $40-45.

The Museum of Speed, located on Ridgewood Avenue (U.S. Highway 1) in South Daytona, was founded by Bill Tuthill, one of the original organizers of NASCAR. The most famous occupant was Sir Malcolm Campbell's record breaking Bluebird V, the fastest vehicle ever to run on the sands of Daytona Beach, which Tuthill rescued from a junkyard in England. The Museum of Speed was a popular attraction for motor car enthusiasts in town for the races. Circa 1950s, $5-7.

New Smyrna, Fla. Old Spanish Shell Mound.

Early Timucua Indians ate oysters and discarded the shells. The shells accumulated into mounds as time passed. In the early 1900s shell from mounds, such as the one shown just south of Daytona Beach, were used in road building and septic tank drains. Cancelled 1909, $6-8.

New Smyrna, Fla.   Stairway to Ancient Fort.

This man stands beside the steps on the south side of the Old Fort Mound in New Smyrna Beach, a few miles south of Daytona Beach. This historic mound and Old Fort ruins have been a mystery for years. Circa 1908, $7-9.

A Brief History of the Postcard

Postcards had their beginning in Austria in 1869. The United States government began to issue postcards in 1873. The cards were stamped on one side to provide for the address and left blank on the other side. The picture postcard did not come into common use in the United States until after 1900. It was about 1902 that the postcard craze hit the country, lasting up to our entry into World War I in the spring of 1917. Collectors would send postcards to total strangers in faraway places, asking for local cards in return. Some collectors specialized in railroad depots, street scenes, cemeteries, churches, courthouses, farms, amusement parks, rivers, steamboats, plants, agricultural products, even comic cards; others collected anything they could find. Postcard albums, bought by the millions, were filled with every sort of postcard ever issued. The craze was actually worldwide, since many countries had postcards.

Before March 1, 1907, it was illegal to write any message on the same side of the card as the address. For that reason the early postcards often have handwriting all over the sides of the picture, and sometimes right across it. Many beautiful cards were defaced in this way. When postcards first started to go through the mails, they were postmarked at the receiving post office as well as that of the sender, making it easy to see the time between post offices—sometimes remarkably brief! The volume of postcards was an important reason for discontinuing the unnecessary second marking about 1910. For years postcards cost only a nickel for six and the postage was a penny, right up to World War II.

The most popular American postcards up to World War I were those made in Germany from photographs supplied by American publishers. At the time of the postcard craze, of course, color photography was still something of a rarity and not commercially viable. For the color cards, black and white photos were touched up, hand-colored, and then generally reproduced by lithography. Lithography consists of transferring the image to a lithographic stone, offset to a rubber blanket, and then printed onto paper. The details in the German produced cards were extremely sharp, and the best of them, technically, have never been matched since.

The German postcard industry folded in the summer of 1914, when the war struck Europe, and never revived. Three years later, the United States entered the war, and the postcard craze ended.

Postcards printed in America were generally of a poorer quality and had a white border. These white border cards were produced until about 1930 when the "linen" textured card was introduced. While this card was less expensive to produce, it also reduced the clarity of detail in the pictures. After 1945 the "chrome" card with a glossy finish replaced the linen card. This type of finish allowed for a very sharp reproduction of the picture. In 1970, a king-sized chrome card (4-inch by 5.875-inch) was introduced and by 1978 it was in general use everywhere.

Bibliography

This is not a complete listing of authors and titles of books on the Daytona Beach area. The aim is to provide a useful guide to further reading. Many of the books listed can be found in Public Libraries in the Daytona Beach area.

Atwell, Cheryl and Vincent Clarida. *Daytona Beach and The Halifax River Area*. Charleston, South Carolina: Arcadia Publishing, 1998.

Barclay, Carolyn, Ceylon Barclay, Don Bostrom, Gordon Kipp and Alice Strickland. *Ormond Beach*. Charleston, South Carolina: Arcadia Publishing, 1999.

Booth, Fred. *Early Days In Daytona Beach, Florida: How A City Was Founded*. (Reprint of a 1951 News-Journal Corporation title "Daytona Beach is Three-Quarters of a Century Old Today.") Daytona Beach: Journal of the Halifax Historical Society, Volume 1, Number 1.

Breslauer, Ken. *50 Years Of Stock Car Racing*. Phoenix, Arizona: David Bull Publishing, 1998.

Cambre, Dale. *Daytona Beach, Florida: A Postcard Tour*. Charleston, South Carolina: Arcadia Publishing, 1998.

Cardwell, Harold D. Sr. *Daytona Beach: 100 Years Of Racing*. Charleston, South Carolina: Arcadia Publishing, 2002.

Cardwell, Harold D., Sr. *Historic Photos of Daytona Beach*. Nashville, Tennessee: Turner Publishing Company, 2007.

Cardwell, Harold D., Sr., and Pricilla D. Cardwell. *Historic Daytona Beach*. Charleston, South Carolina: Arcadia Publishing, 2004.

Cardwell, Harold D., Sr., and Priscilla D. Cardwell. *Port Orange*. Charleston, South Carolina: Arcadia Publishing, 2000.

Cardwell, Sr., Harold D. and Priscilla D. Cardwell. *Port Orange: A Great Community*. Port Orange: City of Port Orange, 2001.

Fitzgerald, T. E. *Volusia County: Past and Present*. Daytona Beach, Florida: The Observer Press, 1937.

Frisbie, Louise K. *Florida's Fabled Inns*. Bartow: Imperial Publishing Company, 1980.

Gaby, Donald Circa *A Brief History of the Halifax Historical Society and Museum*. Daytona Beach, Florida: Self-Published, 1999.

Gaby, Donald Circa *Heaven on the Halifax: A Short History of the Halifax River Yacht Club 1896-2003*. Daytona Beach: Halifax River Yacht Club, 2003.

Gold, Pleasant Daniel. *History of Volusia County, Florida*. Deland: Self-published, 1927.

Hawks, John M. *The East Coast of Florida: A Descriptive Narrative*. Lynn, Massachusetts: Lewis and Winship, Publishers, 1887.

Hebel, Ianthe Bond. *Centennial History of Volusia County, Florida, 1854-1954*. Daytona Beach: College Publishing Company, 1955.

Hinton, Ed. *Daytona: From the Birth of Speed to the Death of the Man in Black*. New York, New York: Warner Books, InCirca, 2001.

Krishef, Robert K. *The Daytona 500*. Minneapolis, Minnesota: Lerner Publications, 1978.

Lazarus, Bill. *The Sands of Time: A Century of Racing at Daytona*. Daytona Beach, Florida: International Speedway Corporation and NASCAR, 2004.

Liston, Broward. *Waves of Challenge: A History of the Daytona Beach/Halifax Area*. Dallas, Texas: Taylor Publishing Company, 1996.

Luther, Gary. *History of New Smyrna*. New Smyrna Beach, Florida: Luther Publishing, 2001.

Mauk, Jonathan V. *The Gallery Of Legends Book*. Daytona Beach, Florida: International Speedway Corporation, 1955.

Merrick, H. James. *Bravo, Stanley!* Kingfield, Maine: The Stanley Museum, InCirca, 2006.

Neely, William. *Daytona U.S.A.* Tucson, Arizona: Aztex Corporation, 1979.

Pope, Maria Davidson. *Remembrances of an Early Daytona Childhood*. Daytona Beach, Florida: self-published, 1977.

Sammons, Sandra Wallus and Jo Anne Sikes. *Edgewater*. Charleston, South Carolina: Arcadia Publishing, 2005.

Schene, Michael G. *Hopes, Dreams, and Promises: A History of Volusia County, Florida*. Daytona Beach: News-Journal Corporation, 1976.

Strickland, Alice. *Ormond-On-The-Halifax*. Ormond Beach, Florida: Self-published, 1980.

Strickland, Alice. *Ormond's Historic Homes*. Ormond Beach, Florida: Ormond Beach Historical Trust, InCirca, 1992.

Strickland, Alice. *The Valiant Pioneers*. Coral Gables: University of Miami Press, 1963.

Sweet, Lawrence J. *New Smyrna Beach*. Charleston, South Carolina: Arcadia Publishing, 2006.
The Odyssey Of An American School System: Volusia County Schools-1854 To 2000. DeLand: Volusia County Schools, 2000.

Tucker, Tom and Jim Tiller. *Daytona: The Quest for Speed*. Daytona Beach, Florida: The News-Journal, 1994.

Tuthill, William R. *Speed on Sand*. Ormond Beach: Ormond Beach Historical Trust, 1978.

Tuthill, William R., Don Bostrom, Carolyn Jernigan, Gordon Kipp, and Ellen Rabin. *Speed on Sand: Revised Edition*. Ormond Beach: Ormond Beach Historical Trust, 2002.

Watson, Henry B. *Bicentennial Pictorial History of Volusia County*. Daytona Beach: News-Journal Corporation, 1976.

Index